Women in Agriculture

Breaking the Grass Ceiling

Research Team

Principal Researchers:

Ashok Khandelwal
Shipra Deo

Senior Researcher:

Dhivya David

Field Coordinators:

Subhash Yadav – *Pratapgarh*
Ashok Kumar Singh – *Agra*
Firoz Khan – *Shahjahanpur*

Surveyors:

Shanti Mishra
Urmila Shukla
Shyama Pandey
Akhtari Bano
Kamla Singh

Women in Agriculture

Breaking the Grass Ceiling

Ashok Khandelwal
Shipra Deo

AAKAR

WOMEN IN AGRICULTURE: Breaking the Grass Ceiling
Ashok Khandelwal and Shipra Deo

First Published, 2013

ISBN : 978-93-5002-242-9

Published by
AAKAR BOOKS
28 E Pocket IV, Mayur Vihar Phase I, Delhi 110 091
Phone : 011 2279 5505 Telefax : 011 2279 5641
info@aakarbooks.com; www.aakarbooks.com

Printed at
Mudrak, 30 A, Patparganj, Delhi 110 091

Contents

Acknowledgements

This study could not have been successfully complete without the invaluable contribution of a large number of people with a wide array of skill and expertise on one hand, and their collective work on the other. We acknowledge the help and thank each one of them. In particular, we extend our special thanks to:

- Alex Pavlovic, the then Managing Director, Sunhara India project for financial and moral support to the idea of conducting the present study.
- The team of researchers, field coordinators and surveyors.
- Ranjit Singh Panwar for entering the data and helping in its analysis.
- All the people who helped in organizing group discussions in the villages or with the officials in field and who helped facilitate our work in many other ways.
- Sandra Bunch, Katty Allen, Lindsey Jones and Mark Sevier who took pains to read the draft report and provided critical suggestions.
- Our publisher Mr K.K. Saxena of Aakar books, Delhi and Padmamalini G. Rao for editing the book.
- All the women who spared time for us to answer questions, participate in the discussions and share their live experiences despite, in many instances, it being a painful emotive journey for them.
- Our spouses and daughters for their unstinted constant support and help.

Preface

One of the most debated contemporary issues in the arena of agriculture relates to participation of women in agriculture. It has drawn the attention of planners, administrators, social workers and academics alike. The debate has captured wide ranging issues from diverse perspectives. It is as much the outcome of changing employment structure within agriculture and structure of economy as it is the changes in the status of women.

Participation of women in agriculture operations has been a historical fact. They are part of the all-important agriculture operations from sowing to harvesting to processing and marketing, though the nature and extent of their involvement depends on the variation in the family/social labour use patterns and agro-production systems. Estimates suggest that the contribution of women in agriculture in India varies from about 50 to 60 per cent in general to above 80 per cent in some specific areas. However, despite this substantial contribution, due to the prevalent social norms and gender inequalities, women farm workers do not get proper recognition.

In the recent past, the role of women in agriculture in India has increased to the extent that the phenomenon has been termed as feminization of agriculture. Studies suggest that the role of women in agriculture has increased in India due to several factors like un-remunerative agriculture, migration for survival and better opportunities, dwindling size of holdings, cash needs, et cetera.

Many development organizations are developing programs with women at focus. However, the mainstream social institutions continue to ignore in large measure their identity and their presence as independent farmers. This restricts their ability to realize their potential as farm workers, as managers, as entrepreneurs and above all, as humans.

Women's lives are determined by a matrix of social and cultural determinants which lead to denial of rights and opportunities for them as independent beings including as farmers. These include their relationship with the spouse, the immediate family, children, village community, government functionaries et cetera. To understand their lives, it is necessary to understand the matrix of relations that encompass women's lives and identify aspects that act as barriers in full realization of their potential.

Lives of women particularly in rural-India cannot be visualized without agriculture and allied activities. As per Census 2011 figures, four out of five women workers in rural India work as agriculture workers as owner cultivators or wage workers.

This research monograph is about women farmers-women who are engaged primarily in cultivation of vegetables and fruits and predominantly belong to small and marginal land holdings. It is the outcome of a baseline survey done in the year 2010–11 in three districts of Uttar Pradesh as part of an action intervention project.

Based on the survey findings, it discusses the structural and other factors that promote and perpetuate gender inequality and prevent women from realizing their full potential as farmers, presents the struggles, positive experiences and practices, explores possible interventions at different levels for different stakeholders, and suggests a framework keeping the women's agency at centre stage while simultaneously enhancing their well being.

There are eight chapters in the book. Chapter 1 lists the issues, includes objectives and describes the methodology and limitations. Chapter 2 provides a synoptic view of the issues women farmers face on the basis of secondary data. Chapter 3 to 6 discuss the survey findings. The summary of findings and recommendations along with constraints and opportunities and an interventions frame for the women farmers to move ahead are provided in Chapter 7.

The main findings in chapter 3 to 6 may appear independent and discreet but they actually are not. The relationships with one another becomes obvious when considered along with various aspects of life-education, ownership of assets, division of work, domestic violence, gendered restrictions, barriers, potential, contestation, objective and subjective conditions, as part of a web of social relations that impact each other.

Chapter 3 provides insights into the material conditions of the sample households in terms of demographic characteristics, education profile, asset base, living conditions, et cetera. The findings suggest the generalized relative deprivation despite being the producers of cash crops.

Chapter 4 discusses the present status of institutional barriers women face as also the bases and processes of these socially constructed barriers, the way they impact women farmers, as well as the struggles of women to break the barriers and realize their potential. These struggles provide the motivation and energy for change. However, overall the observed change is limited and the subjective conditions appear to be weak.

Chapter 5 details the current status of gender-based division of work in agriculture. It suggests, barring exceptions, total male domination of market operations and handling of main equipment and related field-based operations like land preparation and application of fertilizers and pesticides. These operations are relatively less demanding on time but are socially significant. On the other hand, women domination is in labour demanding work of weeding, harvesting, cleaning, et cetera. Some activities are jointly undertaken. The outcome of the secondary position of women observed in chapter 4 is clearly visible in this chapter in terms of work profile and participation in decision-making.

Chapter 6 discusses the role of the State vis-à-vis the existence of women as well as their functions and responsibilities as an agriculturist. It clearly brings out the inadequacy of the State programmes at the level of conception, coverage as well as implementation and gives an impression as if the role of the welfare State is deceptive.

Chapter 7 includes, in addition to a summary of main findings, the wide range of recommendations with an intent of moving towards an agriculture regime that ensures equality, realization of the potential of the women farmers in particular and a better quality dignified life for them.

Finally, Chapter 8 incorporates the outcomes of interventions in one of the districts where an action intervention strategy has been implemented based on the suggested frame of action in Chapter 7.

The outcomes of the action interventions indicate that the strategy suggested has the potential of both empowering and improving conditions of women farmers in question. In the wake of interventions, the women are more confident and assertive, more skilled, have learned new technologies and increased their incomes. More importantly, many have become active promoters and facilitators of social transformation.

We hope that in spite of all its limitations, the people looking for change and strategies for better status of women, be they academicians, administrators, planners or social workers, will find the book of some use.

May 2013

Ashok Khandelwal
Shipra Deo

1

Introduction

The present monograph, as stated in the preface, is based primarily on a baseline field study done in the three districts of Uttar Pradesh as part of an action intervention project. This introductory chapter sets the context and objectives and provides details about the methodology used for the fieldwork and limiting factors.

At the very outset, we wish to spell out our overall development perspective. We are of the belief that in the Indian context, the primary purpose of agriculture should be food security, for which the best model, in our considered opinion, would be of safe decentralized production, procurement, storage and distribution. All other policies should be informed by this. Decentralized local production with appropriate backward and forward linkages is fundamental to sustainable and equitable development. The role of women has to be central in this. Paradigm shift is required in the current development model which is based on betting on the strong and the trickle-down theory. And simultaneously the status of women needs qualitatively change.

It would be pertinent to note here that given the continued agrarian crisis and consequent food insecurity, the Government of India appointed a National Commission for Farmers in 2004 under the renowned agricultural scientist, Prof. M.S. Swaminathan. The first term of reference of the Commission was, 'Workout a comprehensive medium-term strategy for food and nutrition security in the country in order to move towards the goal of universal food security over time'.

1.1 The Context

The problems of Indian agriculture in general and small and marginal farmers in particular are well researched, documented and discussed. We wish not to recount them here. This section merely flags the core issues related to India- agriculture and women in agriculture.

1.1.1 Agricultural Policies and Food Security

Farming in India has undergone unprecedented crises in the recent past.[1] The relative poverty of agricultural workers reflects in the fact that agriculture makes up roughly 16 per cent of national revenue despite being the primary livelihood for more than two-thirds of rural India and more than half of India.[2] Per capita production of essential items like pulses and oil is coming down. Farmers' shrinking land holdings and dependence on increasingly volatile markets has aggravated the crises, increasing poverty levels of the majority of farming community. The State has many programmes like land development programmes, facilities for credit and quality seeds, extension services, irrigation and other inputs at reasonable prices but the majority of farmers remain deprived of these. Additionally, the last six decades of agricultural development policies have not helped resolve the interrelated issues affecting farm productivity and food insecurity like crop insurance, environmental degradation, withdrawal of state support and plateauing of crop yields.

The combined effect of policy, volatile markets and lack of state support greatly hinders agriculture production and farmers' chances of improving their economic and nutritional situations. Small and marginal farmers, including women farmers, have been reeling under the cumulative impact of distorted farm policies over the last five decades. From creation of irrigation facilities to effective reach of extension services and farm subsidies to marketing facilities, the policy arena has consistently favoured larger, commercial farmers. Only a small minority of middle and rich farmers have been assisted since India's predominant model of agricultural development has hinged on betting on the strongest. Increases in food production have been at the expense of increased regional inequalities as well as inequalities at household levels.[3]

1.1.2 Women in Agriculture

Historically, women, in addition to domestic work, have played a significant and important role in agriculture in India, from sowing of seeds and weeding to harvesting of crops. Their involvement varies according to the labour use patterns and agro-production systems in each district and state. Prevalent social norms and gender inequalities arising due to ownership, access and control over resources and decisions, position men and women differently within farming operations on the one hand and do not recognize and value women's work on the other. This secondary status is the social cost women pay.

The social cost of agriculture for women, of late, has been accentuated by 'feminization of agriculture'. With farming no longer a favoured vocation for able-bodied men, women's participation in agriculture has increased, especially in the case of small and marginal farmer households. They are now involved in more farm activities and bear the burden of the most tedious and labour-intensive farm activities, such as weeding and harvesting, which have fallen more and more on women as former male farm workers migrate seasonally/daily to urban areas for livelihood and better wage opportunities.

Generally, this change has not served women, in terms of ownership of land, involvement in decision-making processes, reduction in labour time use and drudgery of work. Conversely, they are more burdened with work than before. Unskilled and disempowered on several counts, women's participation in agriculture has serious implications for women in terms of both agency and well-being.

Indian agriculture is thus confronted with a serious challenge: how to address the issues related to agency and well-being of women farmers. It is against this macro background that the present study has been undertaken.

1.2 Study Objectives

This study's broad objective is to understand the pattern and implications of participation in agriculture of women farmers within the existing gender-relations at the household and community levels. It also examines the role of State vis-a-vis women farmers and attempts to understand perceptions, awareness, attitudes, beliefs and practices of women farmers with a purpose to plan interventions for a better life. The specific objectives are as under.

1.2.1 *Understand Extent and Nature of Participation of Women in Agriculture*

The study looks at the level of participation of women in agriculture in the selected areas within prevailing social dynamics. Perceptible social changes are taking place in Indian society. Agriculture has gone through significant changes as has male-female relationships within and outside the household. Therefore, this study attempts to understand the current status of gender-based division of work and decision-making processes in relation to agricultural work.

1.2.2 *The Nature of Structural Factors that Promote Gender Inequality and Prevent Women from Realizing Their Potential*

The other important objective is to understand the institutional factors that are behind gender biases that work against women agricultural workers. The term 'agricultural workers' includes both cultivators and agricultural wage labourers. In the present study, we are concerned with cultivators and not the wage-workers. The terms 'cultivators' and 'farmers' have been used interchangeably. The traditional influences like caste, religion and patriarchy are rarely homogeneous. The study attempts to understand the nature of land ownership, means of production and its relationship to women's contributions and the subjugation of women in the study area.

1.2.3 *Impact of State Interventions on Woman Farmers*

There have been several initiatives by the State to improve conditions of women farmers in particular. One of the objectives of the present study include assessment of State programmes covering all aspects of their lives in general and agriculture related functions in particular.

1.2.4 Possible Interventions at Different Levels for Different Stakeholders

Inequality breeds contestation. Women fight against intolerable inequalities and biases on a regular basis. The last important objective is to explore the type, intensity and impact of such struggles, and based on overall understanding, to sugget a general plan of action including policy advocacy and specific project mode interventions. The target group for such interventions would be diverse with special focus on women farmers and their families.

1.3 Methodology

1.3.1 The Area

Three districts of UP, each in different zones in the state, were chosen for fieldwork: Agra, Pratapgarh and Shahjahanpur. In each district, three villages were selected for the study. In each village, 20 women farmers were interviewed and eight focus group discussions (FGD) were held. Seven individual interviews were also conducted.

1.3.2 Selection of Villages, Households, Groups, Individuals

(i) Selection of Villages: Three villages from each district were selected on the following criteria: (a) distance from the district headquarters, (b) community composition and (c) the level of marginalization. Attempts were made to ensure proportionate representation of all the major communities in the selected villages.

(ii) Selection of Households: 180 households were selected in nine villages spread over three districts. From each village, 20 households were selected using the snowball sampling method. An eligible household was identified and their members were interviewed. The same household then helped identify other households where women work on the farm. This process was continued until the desired numbers of households (20) were covered. Care was taken that all the selected households were not only involved in horticulture production but also represented women that were either managers of their farms, unpaid workers or equal or near equal partners in agriculture production. Variation in terms of education of the head of the household and size of the farm was also taken into account.

(iii) Selection of Groups for Field Group Discussions (FGD): A total of 24 focus group discussions were conducted with eight in each district. Focus group discussions were held with women farmers, husbands and men from the same households; elderly women farmers, community opinion leaders, and adolescent boys and girls. In each group, six to nine people participated. Opinion leaders with a distinct social status, respected person or social worker or both, were selected for more in-depth interviews.

(iv) Selection of Individuals: In total, 20 individuals were interviewed. In each district, six to seven individuals representing different stakeholders were interviewed. They included: agricultural extension officers from each district, three in all; one NGO in each district, three in all; one representative of a women's organization in each of the three districts, a total of three persons; one senior officer in each district (DM/ADM/WCD officer), three in all; one mandi agent in each village, three in total. In addition to these, local elected representatives, officials and women farmers were also interviewed to get village level information.

1.3.3 *Data Type and Methods of Data Collection*

The study is primary data-based. The primary data was collected through: interviews of the women farmers; individual detailed interviews (IDI) of select people; focus group discussions (FGD) and; case studies. Case studies included typical cases of discrimination, experiences of extreme gender bias, community role models, protests and general struggles. Some secondary data was collated from government sources, mostly from tehsil and district offices.

1.3.4 *Instruments*

Several instruments were developed and pre-tested before canvassing. The instruments developed included: questionnaire for the women farmers; separate FGD guidelines for diferent groups like women and men farmers, opinion leaders and so on; FGD data sheets; interview schedules for AEO, NGO workers, lekhpal and sarpanch.

1.4 Limitations

The area and sample of the study is quite small and thus it may not be appropriate to make State-level generalizations based on the current set of data.

The village women interviewed had never taken part in any sort of interview previously. Explaining the purpose of the interview and rephrasing the language of questions at certain points was a challenge for our investigators.

The focus group discussions usually took two to four hours. At times, it was very difficult to engage women for such a long duration.

Occasionally, men in the village wondered why agriculture-related conversations were being held with women. Investigators had to explain to them that they specifically wanted answers from women.

2

Women in Agriculture: Status and Issues

Of late, the question of women in agriculture has been widely researched and discussed at all levels (regional, national and international) and by all concerned (academics, administrations, politicians, social workers et cetera). Vast literature is available on the subject. This chapter is not a review of the existing literature, rather it provides a synoptic view of the main issues as a backdrop to the field study findings included in next four chapters–chapters 3 to 6. It draws heavily on the official data and reports of the statutory and special commissions set up by the government of India on the issues of women in general and in agriculture in particular. Broadly, the data and studies referred to are from Census, National Sample Survey Organisation (NSSO), National Commission for Women (NCW) and National Commission for Farmers (NCF). Some select references have been provided.

2.1 Farmers in Rural India

Agriculture in India is in a serious crisis. The fact that it has failed to meet the primary purpose of ensuring food security to a large number of those who work in agriculture validates this. The primary producer is often confronted with food insecurity and abysmal living conditions. Despite decades of fast economic growth,[4] food insecurity has reached a critical stage with the Prime Minister of India calling the state of malnutrition in India a 'national shame'[5] and lakhs of farmer having committed suicides.[6] About 78 per cent of the Indian population lives on a paltry daily expenditure of Rs. 20 or less per day.[7]

As per latest NSSO data, in the year 2004–05, India has an estimated 166 million farmers with 86 per cent considered small and marginal, that is, owning up to two hectares of cultivable land. The National Commission for Enterprises in the Unorganized Sector (NCEUS) conducted a detailed examination of these farmers based on a NSSO report (NSSO, 2004), (see NCEUS, Chapters 7 and 9). The results indicate that the level of production from marginal farmers is barely sufficient to feed their households. Consequently, many turn to wage labour or bank on loans for additional income for living expenses and input costs for the next crop cycle. Small and marginal farmers use rented equipment which adds to their cost of production. Most have no access to quality inputs or relevant technical knowhow for application. Testing facilities for soil, fertilizers and pesticides are hardly available. Similarly, access to insurance and credit facilities are almost negligible.

The lack of a level playing field for farmers in the global market regime has further accentuated the crisis, as it greatly affects small farmers adversely due to increased dependence on high cost inputs like seeds, and declining support by the state. With this in mind, the National Policy for Farmers was revised in 2007 with an emphasis on improving farmers' well-being instead of focusing solely on productivity.[8] The agricultural situation in UP is broadly similar to the national scenario.

2.2 Women in Agriculture

Women's place in agriculture in India can be summarized in the following ways:

(a) Development is making agricultural work female-centric across all locations, a phenomenon termed as feminization of agriculture.

(b) The feminization of agriculture is leading to labour intensification for women.

(c) Women continue to remain marginalized and subordinated.

(e) Roles and conditions may have changed for women, but the change lacks quality and pace.

Men that were formerly farm workers are now migrating in urban areas seasonally and/or daily for sustenance or for better opportunities, increasing women's responsibilities in agriculture. But these changes have not led to women's increased ownership of land, increased women's involvement in decision-making processes, shifts in labour time use or decreased drudgery of work. Consequently, women are more burdened with work than before. The shift in roles has affected the return on investments from the farm adversely (Kelkar, 2009).

2.2.1 *Female Agricultural Workforce*

The NSSO data for the year 2004–05 suggests that the total estimated number of agricultural workers was 259 million, constituting 57 per cent of the total workforce. In rural areas, the number was 249 million which constitutes 73 per cent of the total workforce. Approximately two-thirds of the agricultural workforce comprise of farmers.

Table 2.1a: Share of Women in Agriculture (Percentages)

Category/Year	*1983*	*1987–88*	*1993–94*	*1999–2000*	*2004–05*
In agriculture workforce	40.1	39.3	39.5	38.8	41.6
In total farmers	39.7	39.6	38.6	37.9	41.8

Source: Different rounds of NSSO. Includes both usual principal and subsidiary status.

Women make up 41.6 per cent of the overall agricultural workforce. Within farming communities, they make up a slightly higher 41.8 per cent (Table 2.1a). The percentage of women in agriculture was stagnant from 1983 to 1993 and declined through 1999–2000. In 2004–05, however, it reached the highest level in two decades. Table 2.1b suggests that growth of employment in agriculture was almost three times higher for women compared to men from 1994 to 2005.

Table 2.1b: Growth Rates of Employment in Agriculture by Sex (Rural Areas)

Worker Category/Period	*1983/94*	*1994/05*	*1983/05*
Male	1.5	0.5	1.0
Female	1.2	1.4	1.3

Source: NCEUS p. 112

Table 2.2: Women Workers in India in 2001 and 2011 (in million)

Category	2001 *Number in Millions*	2001 *Per cent Share*	2011 *Number in Millions*	2011 *Per cent Share*
Total women population	494.83	—	586.4	—
Total women workers	127.05	25.68*	149.9	25.56*
Total women main workers	72.65	57.18	89.3	59.57
Total women marginal Workers	54.4	42.82	60.6	40.43
Total women owner Cultivators	41.3	33.29	36.0	24.02
Total women agriculture wage workers	50.09	39.43	61.6	41.09
Total women household industry workers	8.08	6.36	8.6	5.74
Total women other workers	27.57	21.7	43.8	29.22
Total women in organized sector (1999)	4.8	3.78		

Source:
1. For serial numbers 1 to 8, Censuses 2001 and 2011
2. For serial number 9, Tenth Five Year Plan
3. *Percentage to total population
4. All other figures in column 3 and 5 are percentages to total workers.

Table 2.2 provides the census data for the year 2001 and 2011 relating to women workers. Less than 15 per cent of women are full-time workers: 72.65 out of 494.83 million in 2001 and 89.3 out of 586.4 million in 2011. Most of the women workers are engaged in the agriculture sector either as cultivators or wage labourers. However in 2011, the percentage share of agriculture workers against total workers has declined to 65.1 per cent compared to 72.7 on 2001. But their absolute number has increased from 91.39 to 97.6 million. Also, the structure has changed as ratio of wage workers increased from 54.8 to 67 per cent in 2011 compared to 2001. The number of cultivators has declined from 41.3 to 36 million on the other hand.

In terms of percentages, among total women workers in rural India, the share of women owner-cultivators has declined from 41.3 to 24 per cent and that of agriculture wage workers increased sharply from 50 to over 61 per cent. The status of women in agriculture has thus come down. All the women workers except about four in a hundred, are part of the unorganized sector without any income, job, food and health security and maternity and old-age benefits.

Thus, women predominantly work in agriculture, but mainly as marginal workers, wage earners or as unpaid family farm worker. Much of their work is not even considered as an economic activity or is enumerated as marginal work, despite expending substantial labour time.

2.2.2 *Participation of Women in Agricultural Activities*

Women participate in most farm-related activities, from land preparation and sowing to harvesting and occasionally, marketing. The nature and extent of their involvement depends on factors like land ownership, family-specific labour use patterns, the existing agro-production system and their caste, class and religion. Generally, women participate more in field-based activities like seed cleaning and sowing, weeding and harvesting. The on-farm role of women can vary from landless wage workers to managers. In this section, we will examine, based on secondary data, women's allocation of time for different activities and their roles in decision-making across different activities.

(i) Labour Time Use of Women

Studies have estimated that women contribute approximately 55 to 66 per cent of their work per day on agricultural production. A study relating to the mountainous regions of India, for instance, calculated that men worked 1,212 hours a year and women work 3,485 hours a year on one-hectare farms (Shiva, 1991).

Table 2.3: Share of Farm Women in Agricultural Operations

Activity	*Involvement (per cent)*
Land preparation	32
Seed cleaning and sowing	80
Inter cultivation activities	86
Harvesting-reaping, winnowing, drying, cleaningand storage	84

Source: NCW, 2005, p. 11

It has been further noted that; for certain farm activities like processing and storage, women dominate so strongly that male workers, involvement is insignificant (Aggarwal, 2003, as quoted in NCW, 2005, p. 8). Another study suggests that about 60 per cent of agricultural operations like sowing of seeds, transportation of saplings, winnowing and storage of grain are handled exclusively by women, while in other jobs, they share the work with men.

Table 2.4 indicates that women spend almost equal time completing agriculture-related activities and domestic work. This is referred to as the 'double burden' of work and an average work day can last over 15 hours. Livestock-related work is also part of domestic work since rural women are primarily responsible for animal care, grazing, fodder collection, cleaning of animal sheds, processing of milk, et cetera. Studies suggest that women account for 93 per cent of employment in dairy production in India (Kelkar, 2009).

Table 2.4: Time and Energy Use by Activity Type of Women Farmers

Activities	*Duration Hours/Min*	*Energy-K. Cal*	*Percentage Time*
Domestic activities	7.55	903	40.53
Agriculture and allied activities	7.00	283	39.69
Sleep	6.50	284	12.76
Rest and recreation	2.15	155	6.97
Total	23.20	2255	100.00

Source: Ibid, p. 12.

It is well-known that women are overburdened but little has been done to reduce the burden. In fact, their workload is increasing despite scientific and technological developments in farm and household equipment. Most of the labour-saving tools and machinery developed are used by men. 'While being an integral and crucial part of the agricultural system, women do not have an access to new agricultural technologies that could save them a tremendous amount of time and back breaking labour' (Cherian et al., 2000).

Women farmers in India are becoming increasingly involved in the agricultural sector but without any recognition not only as farmers but even as workers (compare the two figures of women's daily schedule and census figures of women workers given above). The Draft Policy on Women Farmers prepared by the National Commission for Women (NCW, 2008) aptly sums-up:

> Women's pivotal role in agriculture has never been recognized fully. They work as female agricultural labourers, as farmers, co-farmers, family labourers and (with male out-migration, widowhood, etc.) as managers of the farm and farm entrepreneurs. Women in agriculture refer not only to women agricultural labourers and farmers but also to women working in the various sub-sectors of agriculture and allied non-farm work.

(i) Decision-making Process

While women are active in farm activities, they are rarely involved in decision-making processes. This varies, however, across regions and communities. Recent studies reveal that there is variation across states in India and across farm sizes. Participation in decision-making could take three distinct forms: on the one side, there may not be any participation of women in decision-making while on the other extreme, women may take all the decisions independently; and finally, it may be a joint process wherein both men and women participate equally. The process of decision-making varies across different activities within a household as well.

In the case of agricultural households, especially in north India, the decision-making is by and large controlled by men.

The data set on the decision-making process reveals that independent decision-making by women is more prominent in hilly states like Uttarakhand, where men have migrated for long periods. The least participation was recorded in north Indian states like Haryana. For example, in the case of sowing, sale of produce and buying farm land, decisions made independently by women in Haryana was 20, 22 and 33 per cent respectively. For Uttarakhand, the percentage points for the three respective operations were 62, 63 and 62 per cent (ICAR, 2004).

Table 2.5: Decision-Making in Agricultural Activities (by Per cent)

Decision Item	*Male*	*Female*	*Joint*
Adoption of high yielding varieties	83	-	17
Use of fertilizers/pesticides	80	-	20
Purchase of agricultural equipment	72	-	28
Procurement of credit	50	0	50
Selling of crops/cereals/vegetables	32	6	62

Source: Bala, 2003 (Reproduced from NCW 2008, p. 203)

Micro field studies also show men's control over decision-making. One study suggests that male members did seek consent from women but their suggestions and/or objections were not taken into account (NCW, 2005, pp. 18–21). Results of a study done in Himachal Pradesh are included in Table 2.5. It suggests that, even in a state where women are in the forefront of decision-making due to mass migration of men, they are still not involved in agriculture-related decision-making. In *Invisible Activities of Rural Women,* author Sarmishta Chaudhary refers to another study conducted in Orissa, which revealed that farm women did not make any decisions about farm operations independently (Chaudhary, 2004).

2.2.3 *Types of Women Farmers*

As mentioned above, women's position is most often determined by the control she has over means of production and decision-making at various levels. Based on these two criteria, one can identify four kinds of women farmers in Indian agriculture: (1) women farmers as managers; (2) women farmers as equal partners; (3) women farmers as unpaid family labour, and (4) women as paid wage labourers. The variation in the first three categories of farmers is determined primarily by twin factors of decision-making and control over production processes and output. The ownership of productive assets also plays an important role in the process of decision-making and control. In gender terms, the three categories are placed on a continuum. On the two extremes of decision-making and control, there are women managers who have full command over the decision-making and control, and unpaid women farmers who have no involvement in decision-making. Women who are equal partners are in the middle and are not only equally involved in decision-making with men but also have control over process and output as well. The fourth category is different in that these women farm workers have no stake in output. They work according to instructions from the employers. The duration of labour is determined by the employers and they are compensated for their time.

Ownership, decision-making and control are therefore important factors when examining the status of women in agriculture. The extent, depth and nature of women's involvement in their households is of vital importance. In India, a large number of women fall into the fourth category and are wage labourers. The next largest group is in category three. These women work on family farms but are neither involved in decision-making nor have any control over output. The two together include the majority of women agricultural workers. Yet, there is an emerging category of independent farmers due to migration and widowhood, but they too are constrained because of barriers like ownership of land title and social barriers that practice seclusion. The second category of joint decision-makers is found but, again, in small numbers. The transition from third and fourth categories to first and/or second category therefore remains a major issue.

2.2.4 Outcomes of Women's Participation in Agricultural Work

(i) Double Work Burden

One outcome of women's participation in agricultural work, the double work burden, has already been referred to. Besides ill-health of women, it has several other implications. The work burden acts as a motivator for women to have many children so that they can help in daily chores from a young age (NCW, 2008). The oldest girl may be forced to skip school if there are younger siblings to take care of, negatively affecting the oldest girl's future. This phenomenon is quite common in large parts of rural India, especially north India.

(ii) Adverse Impact on Agricultural Output

The other outcomes have bearing for both families and agricultural output. One type of implication is contradictory, positive in one way and negative in other instance. Since women work in both arenas, and the capacity to work is restricted, there is a substitution effect of one work on the other. When a household grows a labour-intensive cash crop, the additional labour input by women increases crop output and is seen as a beneficial effect of women's participation, although she may not make any related decisions. However, the (same) heightened level of participation by women may be a loss for a small child who needed his or her mother's care but was deprived owing to her investing more labour-time in agriculture. However, the agricultural outcomes are not dependent on labour input alone.

When a woman has to participate in agricultural production because her husband has migrated, she may fail to take appropriate decisions or to mobilize required resources in agriculture. Such participation may even be disastrous for the family, bringing distress and tensions (Hardikar, 2004). Generally speaking, gender inequalities affect rural and agricultural development adversely, and therefore, if the participation of women has a gender-equal effect, then only are the pay offs for society, household and the women concerned considered positive (Agarwal 2003; Kelkar, Nathan and Walter, 2003; FAO 2006).

(iii) Unequal Wages

Wages differ for women workers in agriculture. On average, women's wages are much lower than men's for the same work. According to the NSSO data, the men's wages are higher for all the agricultural operations. For instance, for ploughing, the daily wages for men are 66.10 rupees, and for women are 42.16 rupees. The lowest wage differential is for harvesting, at 55.67 and 45.67 respectively. For weeding, the wages are relatively even more, 51.23 vs. 43.26. Overall, the ratio of female wage to male wage rate is constant over the years, 1993–94 to 2004–05, at around 0.7 (NCEUS. p. 123, Table 8.1).

(iv) Well-being versus Agency

Broadly speaking, positive outcomes relate to either well-being and/or agency. If a woman's participation in agriculture leads to a better life situation for her, it impacts her well-being. On the other hand, if participation leads to personality development, better self-image and assertion, it impacts her agency. Agency impact is seen when the participation is in terms of managers or co-managers. It is also related to the ownership and control of means of production, and status of women as discussed in the next section.

2.3 Important Issues

2.3.1 Social Location of Women

In the words of Dr. M.S. Swaminathan (Quoted from NCW, 2008, p. 9), noted farm scientist, 'Some historians believe that it was women who first domesticated crop plants and thereby initiated the art and science of farming. While men went out hunting in search of food, women started gathering seeds from the native flora and began cultivating those of interest from the point of view of food, feed, fodder, fibre and fuel.' Thus, historically the role of women in the survival of human beings is fundamental. They also enjoyed social status in accordance with their contribution and roles. But gradually, the situation of women changed. Their roles got restricted and they became domesticated. Their social status got lost and their identity got merged with other significant ones. The rule of patriarchy was established and women became subjugated.

Despite their valuable contribution, women to-day are at a disadvantage in the final analysis because they are usually rendered insignificant when it comes to decision-making and more so when it comes to sharing of output or fruits of labour. They typically have minimal or no control over the resources generated.

Gender inequality has wide repercussions at different levels. Some of these have already been discussed here: Double work burden, domestication and violence against women are well-known outcomes. Less known are social and economic implications in public spaces. From an agricultural point of view, there is a large body of evidence suggesting that gender inequalities affect rural and agricultural development adversely and deepen the agricultural crisis and food insecurity in India. (Agarwal 2003; FAO 2006).

The subjugation or secondary position of women stems from two basic causes: lack of effective ownership of land and seclusion. These material conditions and norms form the base of gender inequality. These two aspects and their implications are briefly discussed below.

(i) Land Ownership

Social and cultural gender norms change when women acquire control of land and property assets.

> My fieldwork findings (in connection with production networks, microfinance and sex trafficking) in rural areas in Bangladesh, India and Nepal suggested that women's control over assets or land results into effectively breaking the vicious circle of poverty-patriarchy- illiteracy-ill health, including HIV infection. With independent land rights, women are able to address the local world of male dominance, and of stigma and humiliation in case of any transgression of the gender norms (Kelkar, 2009).

Land ownership in India overwhelmingly favours men. The NSSO data for the year 1999–2000 related to landholding pattern of female-headed households, for instance, reveals that 90.9 per cent of such households own less than one hectare and

96.5 per cent up to two hectares. The ownership of land is a crucial factor in determining the status of women in general and within agriculture in particular. A study conducted by Oxfam on the status of women farmers in Uttar Pradesh, for instance, shows that only six per cent of women own land, less than one per cent participate in government training programmes, four per cent have access to institutional credit and only eight per cent have control over agricultural income.

Effective land rights for women would aid overall development and would have a positive impact on welfare, efficiency, equality and empowerment. There is direct benefit in terms of crops, fodder, trees, vegetable gardens, livestock, et cetera and indirect advantages include bargaining power, gain help/support, access to credit, social status, et cetera (Agarwal, 1998, pp. 27–30). There are, for instance, several studies suggesting that gender inequality has implications for children's education and nutrition and the household's food security. One reason for this is that men are less concerned with household requirements and spend more money on their personal requirements. Women, on the other hand, spend income on their family's general consumption [Mencher, 1988]. Ensuring women and men have equal land and asset rights would increase economic opportunities, encourage investment in land and crop production, improve household food security and enhance women's agency, leading to better agricultural management.

The need to extend land ownership to women has been articulated by agriculture scientists as well.

> A recent analysis of the state of Indian farmers by the National Commission on Farmers (NCF) emphasized that lack of title to land makes it difficult for women farmers to access institutional credit. For example, barely five per cent of women seemed to have been issued with Kisan credit cards out of the many millions with whom such cards have been issued. Extension and input supply services also do not reach women at the right time and place. Therefore, as stressed by the NCF, there is need for a new deal for women in agriculture. (Swaminathan, 2005).

Rural poverty is deeply rooted in the imbalance between

what women do and what they possess (ILC and IFAD, 2004). Lack of effective ownership is a major social barrier for women to realize their potential. The importance of land ownership for women farmers has not only been highlighted by scores of studies, but has been articulated by women themselves. Women consider this crucial, as shown by the voices of women from the field (Box: 2.1). Ownership will provide opportunities for better agricultural production as it would provide access to inputs like credit, seeds, water, et cetera. Secondly, it would also help women in raising their voices against domestic violence as they would be less dependent on men and ideally, would be able to assert themselves and oppose injustices.

BOX 2.1: Voices from the Field

(i) Land (like other productive assets) is an opportunity for change. It is a way to have access to other resources, such as water, seeds, new technologies and bank loans.
(ii) When we earn our own money, we are less frightened of arguing with our husbands, on spending decisions.
(iii) If our husbands want us to eat, then we eat, it totally depends on them. If the land were in my name, he would no longer beat me, and he would take care of the children as well.

Source: ILC and IFAD, 2004

In Andhra Pradesh, women's groups have leased land through money borrowed from self-help groups. The importance of land for women is aptly reflected in the following statement by women, 'We had tongues but could not speak, we had feet but could not walk. Now that we have the land, we have the strength to speak and walk' (Quoted in Agarwal, 1998, p. 40.)

(ii) Seclusion

Seclusion means domestication, the worst form of seclusion practised in north India. One instrument of seclusion is the veil system or *Parda Pratha*.[9] This system restricts and controls women's movement. The women are rendered fully dependent on men because of the practice. The social norm of *parda* implies that women are not free to step outside the house and therefore cannot do marketing, cannot receive an education and so on. Thus, there is a different social role specification for men and women. The prevalent social norms and gender inequalities position men and women differently in the agriculture activities. We have noted these gender based differences in agriculture-related work earlier in this chapter. In fact, role specification spans almost across every walk of life.

The differences between men and women, due to roles and responsibilities, ownership of resources and assets, access to education, time use, mobility, and patterns of control over income, contribute to gender segmentation in agriculture and preclude women from deriving full benefits of their involvement in agriculture. The gender-based roles cut across religion, regions, cultures, races, age, colour and so on. However, there is a perceptible variation in the situation from absolute domination with negligible rights to semblance to equal rights. There could indeed be cases of women domination as well. Such cases are of course exceptions and are the outcomes of patriarchy itself when a woman acts like a man. The variations in men-women relationships naturally cut across communities, castes, households, occupations and time. Variations are found in agricultural work as well.

Women's status is historically determined but is not static, though the direction and pace of changes are not similar. Women's status is diverse within India. But women have a secondary status to men, which is well established. This is reflected in the fact that most of the work they do, the household work, is not counted as an economic activity.

2.3.2 *Feminization of Agriculture*

The relative share of women in agriculture is increasing over time. Earlier we noted that women workers grew three times faster compared to men. Further, Table 2.6 suggests that percentage share of main male agriculture workers has significantly declined from 80.4 to 65.2 during 1977–78 to 2009–10. The corresponding decline in case of women workers is much less from 88.1 to 79.4. In other word, the female–male ratio of main farm workers has, over the same period, increased from about 107 to 126.

The feminization process has two aspects that need exploration: the reasons for increased participation of women and the change in the nature of work that women do. Studies suggest several reasons for women's increased role in agriculture. Kelkar (2009) finds the phenomenon linked with a variety of factors, such as male out migration, the growing number of households headed by women and the development of labour-intensive cash crops. The most important direct explanation is that agriculture is no more remunerative and less attractive for several reasons like dwindling landholdings.

Agriculture is a less paying employment for majority of farmers is widely recognized and is primary reason for feminization. It reflects in the income inequality between agriculture and other sectors. And this sector gap is widening at an increasing rate forcing men to find jobs elsewhere[10]. The non-remunerative agriculture and lack of employment opportunities in the rural areas act as a major push factor for migration, circular migration in particular.

Table 2.6: Share of Agriculture Workers per 1000 by Sex-Rural Areas

NSSO Round	*Year*	*Male(m)*		*Female(f)*		*f/m ratio*
		Main Workers	*All Workers*	*Main Workers*	*All Workers*	*Main Workers*
66	2009–10	625	628	789	794	126.24
61	2004–05	662	665	814	833	122.96
55	1999–00	712	714	841	854	118.12
50	1993–94	737	741	847	862	114.93
43	1987–88	739	745	825	847	111.64
38	1983	772	775	862	875	111.66
32	1977–78	804	806	868	881	107.96

Source: NSSO Report no. 537 (NSSO, 2011)

That many men do not want to pursue agriculture work anymore is a well documented fact. One senior officer in UP observes:

> Out of an estimated number of 22.15 million rural households in Uttar Pradesh, 77.4 per cent are farmer households. According to data released by NSSO (59th round), 24 per cent of UP farmers (27 per cent at all India level) did not like farming and felt that agriculture was not profitable. In all 41 per cent farmers in UP (40 per cent at all India level) felt that, given a choice, they would take up some other career. This indicates a serious problem wherein the main protagonist is suffering from low self-esteem and does not believe that what he is doing is worthwhile economically or even socially. In the social hierarchy, farming as a profession now figures considerably low in the social order (Kumar, 2005).

Thus, conditions in agriculture drive the mass of small and marginal male farmers out, seeking a livelihood.[11] The family remains in the village clinging to a small piece of land. It has been argued that this circular migration[12] is distress migration as people are forced into it (Deshingkar & Start, 2003).

This process of seasonal migration in recent times has accentuated due to LPG (Liberalization, Privatization and Globalisation) based development model. As part of this development model, state subsidies were reduced, leading to an agrarian crisis. In addition, increased use of technology has led to less employment generation overall. Acquisition of land for various purposes like roads, industrial projects, housing, dams, sanctuaries, et cetera have rendered hundreds of thousands of agricultural families landless.[13] For these reasons, and others, like better employment opportunities elsewhere, the phenomenon of circular migration has increased considerably. Consequently, the role of women in agriculture has increased. This increasing role of women in agriculture has been termed, to repeat, as a feminization of agricultural work.

The changes in the nature of work done by women, as discussed in Section 2.2, is by and large related to the status of women in society. The micro studies suggest that, in some areas, small farms are increasingly managed by women because of male migration. The data related to decision-making in Himachal Pradesh testifies to this. The increased participation of women in agriculture impacts the nature of work women do.

2.3.3 *The State and Women in Agriculture*

> The analysis of results from the Farmers' Survey clearly establish that these (small and marginal) farmers have inadequate access to information, to agencies promoting technological change, to cooperative networks and related organizations and are less able to benefit from the plethora of government interventions. (NCEUS, p. 144)

The role of the State in India is determined by the Constitution which guarantees the country's people several fundamental rights. The right to equality (Article 14) and the right to live with dignity and freedom (Article 21) are most important. It also enjoins the government through Directive Principles, to take appropriate measures to ensure adequate means of livelihood, right to work, living wages, education and just and humane conditions of work. Under these constitutional obligations, the State has formed several laws, policies and programmes to ensure gender equality and dignified life for the people of India. There are several such laws, policies and programmes that are relevant for the target group in question. Some of these programmes are listed in Annex C.

Yet, State efforts are highly inadequate in regard to education and extension services. Policies and programmes related specifically to agriculture are not gender-sensitive. The minimal agricultural extension services provided are male-dominated. Similarly, programmes such as land reforms, ration cards, *kisan* cards, and so on, cater mainly to men. Worst of all, women farmers have not been given status of 'farmer' despite the fact that they contribute more to agriculture than men do. Not much attention has been paid to the issues of women in the planning process either. 'Insufficient attention to some work arena, where women are most active, such as cultivation of crops and vegetables, regeneration of degraded forests, wasteland development and watershed development, has shown that women's contributions and concerns remain invisible in planning and thus, are ignored—?' (Sujaya, 2006).[14] The policies and programmes are guided by men's ideology.

It is not surprising, therefore, that no concerted effort has been made to ensure that land rights are in the name of women or are at least jointly named. Even The National Policy for Farmers 2007 (PIB, 2007) reflects this problem. Disappointed with the way women's issues were dealt with in the Policy and that some of the important suggestions given by NCW were left out, the NCW finally developed a Draft Policy for Women in Agriculture, stating, 'It was felt that crucial areas have been left out (in the draft national policy) and these need to be included. (NCW 2008)'

To summarize, there has been no State effort to empower women in agriculture. The approach of the State at the most ends up with providing some relief. Even the newly announced programme of Mahila Kisan Sashaktikaran Pariyojana (for details please see Annexure C) falls far short of empowering women, as it ignores the social constraints. The efforts of the State are indifferent at one level and do not lead to benefits on the other.

2.3.4 *Disadvantaged Women*

We have earlier noted how liberalization has impacted agricultural working conditions. There are several recent changes in agriculture that have affected women farm workers more adversely than men. A study by the NCW summarizes the disadvantages quite comprehensively. These are some of the study's conclusions:

(i) Change in the cropping pattern to horticulture and floriculture due to diminishing land plots has reduced the demand for manual labour in which, women are engaged.Women are excluded from opportunities of livelihood in these new modes of agriculture.

(ii) Diversion of land for non-agricultural purposes such as infrastructure development and setting up of SEZs is leading to widespread loss of livelihood, which is not compensated by other employments that are generated, particularly for women.

(iii) The dwindling forests and erosion of access to the forests has led to loss of livelihood for women particularly from tribal, Dalit, and pastoral communities.

(iv) The policy shift from Universal to Targeted PDS has led to a sharp decline in consumption per capita from just over 2,200 calories per day in 1987–88 to around 2,150 in 1999–2000. The latest NSSO survey suggests further decline in calorie consumption and the widening of the gender gap in malnutrition.

(v) Rising agrarian distress has also led to increase of violence against women. When livelihood and employment have been threatened, discrimination and violence perpetrated on women tends to increase.

2.4 Summary

The majority of farm women belong to small and marginal families. Most of these households are economically poor and socially isolated. Participation of women in agriculture has increased significantly as more men migrate in search of wage labour. In some cases, the demand for labour has increased due to the introduction of labour intensive cash crops.Farm women suffer from a double burden of both domestic and agricultural work. Combined, these two workloads can take almost 15 hours a day.

Women put in more labour than men, yet they hold a secondary position in their households, communities and societies. Women do not own productive or other assets, are rarely involved in decision-making or have control over production or money. The gender inequality in agriculture has social implications. It affects production and agriculture adversely, promotes food insecurity, perpetuates domestic violence and so on.

New and quickly emerging developments in agriculture, especially related to liberalization and commercialization, linkages with international markets and the withdrawal of the State, has led to new issues. The State, however, has been indifferent towards the majority of farmers. This is incongruent with the constitutional obligations of the State. Especially for women in agriculture, the State has not been a source of empowerment. The reach and implementation of programmes is highly inadequate. The impact is negligible, and in some instances, even negative. Concentrated government initiatives are required to: (a) expand the network of institutional credit to cover all the farmers; (b) meet the credit needs of the small and marginal farmers by earmarking credit for the group and ensuring credit in time and according to necessity; (c) focus extension and marketing initiatives on this group; (d) promote awareness and group initiatives; (e) enhance education and skill development; (f) simplify procedural formalities and make them user-friendly, keeping in mind illiteracy; (g) cover these farmers under universal social security providing for health expenses, life and unemployment insurance, maternity benefits and old age pensions.

The goal of gender equality in agriculture is primary and can be achieved if women are given effective control and ownership of land, are technologically empowered, are skilled in enhancing agricultural management, and are imparted with knowledge of agriculture. This should undoubtedly ensure increase in agricultural production and consequently overcome poverty and income inequality. Along with the above measures, a widespread gender sensitization in rural areas through information and communication technologies would help develop a social understanding of women as producers, farmers and economic contributors. In the following chapters, the report will look at the reality of women in agriculture through the findings of the field survey in the three districts of Uttar Pradesh.

3

Socioeconomic Profiles of Sample Populations

This Chapter analyses primary and secondary data to understand the socioeconomic profile of women farmer households. On the basis of primary data, it examines demographic characteristics, production and other asset bases and housing and living conditions of sample families.

3.1 Background of Selected Districts

The census and other official statistics in Tables 3.1, 3.2 and 3.3 show variations in population, population density, sex ratio, urbanization, literacy rates, social categories, area, crop patterns and land size across the three districts. Certain features, such as the level of irrigation and crop density, are relatively similar.

Based on only secondary data, it would be difficult to say as to which district is more developed. There are sets of data that indicate one district is slightly more progressive than the other, while other sets indicate the opposite. In terms of literacy, income and urbanization, Agra is most developed. However, with respect to sex ratio, Pratapgarh takes the lead. In terms of urbanization, Pratapgarh, with little over five per cent, stands nowhere near Agra and Shahjahanpur with more than 43 per cent and 21 per cent respectively. Agra is the most developed economically, reflected in the fact that the percentage of cultivators as main workers is only 31.3 per cent compared to more than 55 per cent in the other two districts.

Table 3.1: Population Characteristics

Item	*Agra*	*Shahjahan-pur*	*Pratap-garh*
Men	19.62	13.39	13.63
Women	16.60	11.26	13.68
Total	36.22	24.65	27.31
Rural population	20.54	19.39	25.87
S.C. population	7.88	4.31	6.01
HH below povertyline (% rural)	71.09		
Urban population 2001 %	43.3	21.3	5.3
Population density per sq km	899	557	735
Sex Ratio-2001	846	841	1004
Literacy rate - Total	62.6	49.2	57.6
Literacy rate - men	74.6	59.8	74.0
Literacy rate - women	48.4	36.4	41.5
Cultivators-main	31.3	55.5	56.7
Agricultural labor-main	8.3	16.7	15.4

Note: Population in 100,000s
Source: Census 2001 as given in statistical abstracts of each District.

Table 3.2 suggests that the three districts differ considerably in agricultural indicators, in both absolute and relative terms.

The net area and percentage of cultivable area varies; the total cultivable area is 80 per cent in Shahjahanpur and only 60 per cent in Pratapgarh. There is, however, comparatively less variation in irrigated areas, with a range of 88 to 94 per cent of net area. Compared to greater India's irrigation level of less than 40 per cent, it is obvious that the three districts of UP enjoy considerably better irrigation facilities. All three districts fall within the command area.[15] Most of the irrigation is channelled through canals. The water table is superior to the Indian average and all the districts have many private bore wells. The area is, therefore, quite favourable for cash crops, including vegetables.

Rows 9-13 in Table 3.2 reveal a direct relation between agricultural productivity and area cultivated with commercial crops. Shahjahanpur and Agra have much higher per hectare value addition as well as a high rate of commercial crop production compared to Pratapgarh. Shahjahanpur has

Table 3.2: Agriculture Details 2007–08

Item	*Agra*	*Shahjahan-pur*	*Pratap-garh*
Total net cultivated area (per 1,000 hectares)	282	350	218
% area cultivable	71	80	60.2
Area cultivated more than once (per 1,000 hectares)	132	263	80
Total area under irrigation (per 1,000 hectares)	254	331	192
Net Irrigated Area of Sown Area (%)	88.2	94.6	88.3
Cropping Intensity	146.8	175	136.2
Canals (Km)	737	892	1,767
Private bores	68,720	104,764	101,739
Area under commercial crop of GCA (%)	39	14.1	5.4
Total production food grains (per 1,000 MT)	598	1487	554
Total potato production (per 1,000 MT)	1,311	181	100
Value addition per hectare of net sown area at current prices (Rs)	52,058	67,293	32,726
Value addition per agriculture worker (Rs)	32,964	NA	NA

Source: Statistical Abstract, District Agra, Shahjahanpur and Pratapgarh. Office of Economics and Statistics

reported highest value addition of Rs. 67,293, despite the fact that Agra has a greater area under commercial crop production. The reason could be the nature of the crops grown. Agra produces more potatoes and wheat, whereas Shahjahanpur produces sugarcane, which sells at a higher value. One of the reasons for low average per hectare realization in Pratapgarh could be the relatively small average size of holdings (see Table 3.3). Pratapgarh has a higher percentage of small and marginal holdings, and the total area under these holdings is greater than the other two districts.

Table 3.3: Land Ownership Patterns 2000-01

Item	*Agra*	*Shahjahan-pur*	*Pratap-garh*
Small and marginal land holdings in total holdings per cent	84.2	89.0	94.2
Area under marginal and small holdings of all area per cent	49.6	59.2	67.6
Average size of marginal holdings in hectare	0.5	0.4	0.3
Average size of all holdings in hectares	1.2	1.0	0.6

Source: Statistical Abstract, District Agra, Shahjahanpur and Pratapgarh. Office of Economics and Statistics

To summarize, in terms of dominant agricultural development indicators, Agra is the most developed district, Shahjahanpur is second and Pratapgarh is third. However, Shahjahanpur has the highest percentage of area irrigated, and per hectare value addition followed by Agra. In terms of sex ratio though, Pratapgarh is first with 1,004. Both Agra and Shahjahanpur are way behind with sex ratios of less than 850. This highlights an uncomfortable, but perhaps true, social reality that development is not inevitably gender friendly. In these examples, with increased development, the sex ratio falls, to the women's disadvantage.

3.2 Demographic and Household Characteristics

3.2.1 Family Size

Data was collected on both nuclear and joint families and showed a range between two-member families, as the smallest family size, to a 22-member family as the largest. About 18 per cent of families reported having ten or more members. About 25 per cent of survey participants reported a family size of up to five members. The mean family size of the sample population is 7.44, which is much higher than the latest national average of five as per the Census and 4.6 as per NSSO.

3.2.2. *Education*

Table 3.4: Education of the Head of the Households

Category	*Shahjahanpur*		*Pratapgarh*		*Agra*		*Total*	
	Number	*%*	*Number*	*%*	*Number*	*%*	*Number*	*%*
Illiterate	28	46.7	15	24.6	17	28.3	60	33.1
Primary	5	8.4	18	29.5	5	8.3	28	15.5
Upper Primary	20	33.4	12	19.7	7	11.7	39	21.5
Sec School	7	11.6	13	21.3	23	38.4	43	28.8
College	0		3	4.9	8	13.4	11	6.1
Total	60		61		60		181	

Source: Source of all the Tables is household surveys unless otherwise stated.

Table 3.5: Education of the Female Survey Participants

Category	*Shahjahanpur*		*Pratapgarh*		*Agra*		*Total*	
	Number	*%*	*Number*	*%*	*Number*	*%*	*Number*	*%*
Illiterate	48	80	42	68.8	48	80	138	76.2
Primary	7	11.7	9	14.8	3	5	19	10.5
Upper Primary	4	6.7	3	4.9	8	13.3	15	8.3
Secondary	1	1.7	5	6.5	1	1.7	5	2.8
College			2	3.3	2	1.1		
Total	60		61		60		181	

One-third heads of households were reported to be illiterate. The best educated district is Pratapgarh; only 24.6 per cent reported having no education. Shahjahanpur has reported the lowest education level, with 46.7 per cent illiteracy. Slightly over six per cent reported education at college level or higher, but none of these were from Shahjahanpur. The highest level of high school education was in Agra, at over ten per cent.

Table 3.5 provides details on the educational status of the female survey participants. A majority of survey participants (76 per cent) reported that they never had any formal education. Compared to heads (33 per cent), who are males, the ratio is very high. Only one out of 181 reported education beyond the secondary school and only seven reported education between the 9th and 12th classes.

The highest level of reported education was from Pratapgarh. However, this was not in line with the findings of secondary data wherein Pratapgarh had the lowest rate of literacy. It seems, therefore, that the sample is biased towards the literate.

Men's education level is almost three times that of women. The gender differences increase with the level of education: the higher the level of education, the greater the difference between men and women.

3.2.3 *Marriage Age*

About ten per cent of survey participants reported that they were married by the age of ten. About half the women survey participants said that they were married between the ages of 14 to 17. The percentage of women who got married after the legal age of 18 is 15 per cent. That means an overwhelming majority of 85 per cent were married younger than the legal age of 18 years.

Table 3.6 : Distribution of Sample Households by Sex of Head

Sex of Head	*Shahjahanpur*	*Pratapgarh*	*Agra*	*Total*
Male	55	56	56	167
Female	5	5	4	14
Total	60	61	60	181

3.2.4 *Distribution of Sample Households by Sex of Head*

Across India, approximately 12 per cent of households are reported to be headed by women. The study sample reports about eight per cent of female-headed households. (See Table 3.6). One reason for the disparity with the national average could be that this study only included agricultural families who have women farmers and are involved in vegetable growing. This could mean that women-headed households are less involved growing vegetable crops. There could be several barriers for women-headed households to raise vegetable crops: the labour intensive nature of the crops, market linkages, et cetera. Keeping in view the small representation of female-headed households, it may not be desirable to have a detailed analysis on the basis of the head of the household.

3.2.5 Occupation

Among the families interviewed, only six per cent reported that agriculture was not a main occupation for anyone in the family. 22.6 per cent of families reported wage labour as the main occupation of the head of the household and another 45 per cent as a secondary occupation. Thus, wage labour is crucial for the majority of the families to survive. This is the reality for most cultivator households in India and is the reason, as discussed in Chapter 2, for feminization of agriculture.

3.3 Distribution of Assets

This section discusses findings related to availability and ownership of various assets. Assets are classified in four main categories: agricultural land, other productive assets, household assets, and residential properties by both the extent of ownership and the type of ownership.

3.3.1 Agricultural Land Ownership

Table 3.7: Land Ownership Pattern by District (per cent)

Land Size in Bighas	*Shahjahanpur*	*Pratapgarh*	*Agra*	*Total*
up to one	11.5	47.5	18.2	26.5
1.01 to 2	17.3	23.7	18.2	19.9
2.01 to 3	11.5	10.2	18.2	13.3
3.01 to 5	17.3	11.9	25.5	18.1
5.01 to 7.5	11.5	3.4	7.3	7.2
7.51 to 10	9.6	3.4	10.9	7.8
10.01 to 15	13.5		1.8	4.8
15+	7.7			2.4
Total	100.0	100.0	100.0	100.0

Among the women interviewed, 91.7 per cent reported that their husbands owned agricultural land. Others reported farming on leased land. The ownership pattern suggests that the land owned is not much, the average size is 3.14 *bighas*. However there is variation in the ownership, both intra and inter districts. The majority falls in the small and marginal category. 75 per cent of families own less than five bighas of land. Pratapgarh farmers own the least agricultural land, whereas Shahjahanpur farmers the most. The individual ownership details of the agricultural land within the households will be discussed in Chapter 4 (section 4.1.1 a).

More than one-third reported leasing land. About 40 per cent of households in Agra and Shahjahanpur reported leasing in land, and 25 per cent in Pratapgarh. Sizes of the land leased in ranged from one quarter of bighas to 20 *bighas*. In Pratapgarh, however, the maximum size of land leased in was four bighas.[16] All the leases are oral and are therefore in violation of the laws of the land; so far as tenancy terms and conditions are concerned. The lease is either on a cash or share basis. In Pratapgarh, the leases are on a share basis. In the other two districts, both types of arrangements exist. However, cash basis is more common in Agra, at about 45 per cent, than in Pratapgarh where it is about 28 per cent. The share basis is 50:50 which is quite high and unfavourable for the person leasing in. Moreover there is no security of lease.

3.3.2 *Ownership of House and Other Assets*

(i) Residential Premises

Except for two households, every household owns homestead land. However, the size of the land varies. Table 3.8 provide details on the ownership of residential premises within the household. Like agricultural land, men primarily own residential land. Over 90 per cent of houses are recorded in the name of male household members. The Pattern is similar across all the districts. Only 6.6 per cènt of residential houses are owned by women. Joint ownership is negligible. It is to be noted here that this percentage is slightly less than the women-headed households in our sample. Pratapgarh has reported the highest percentage (8.2) of women ownership.

Table 3.8: Type of Ownership of Residential Houses

Category	*Shahjahanpur*		*Pratapgarh*		*Agra*		*Total*	
	Number	*%*	*Number*	*%*	*Number*	*%*	*Number*	*%*
Man	55	91.7	55	90.2	55	91.7	165	91.2
Woman	4	6.7	5	8.2	3	5.0	12	6.6
Joint	1	1.7	1	1.6	1	1.7	3	1.7
NA					1	1.7	1	0.6

Table 3.9: Ownership of Assets in the Name of Women

Category	*Shahjahanpur*		*Pratapgarh*		*Agra*		*Total*	
	Number	*%*	*Number*	*%*	*Number*	*%*	*Number*	*%*
Yes	25	41.7	16	26.2	51	85.0	92	50.8
No	35	58.3	45	73.8	9	15.0	89	49.2

(i) Ownership of Other Assets

Slightly more than half (50.8 per cent) of women in the survey responded that they own assets in their name (Table 3.9.) In Agra 85 per cent reported that they own assets in their own name. The lowest figure was for Pratapgarh (26.2 per cent).

On further probing, two-thirds reported ownership of jewellery. Many of them, however, said their right is limited to use of the jewellery and have no right to sell or gift it. For most of them, the jewellery was received at marriage from their parental house. About 13 per cent of women reported ownership of land. This appears to be on the higher side especially when compared to the reported figure related to ownership of cultivated agriculture land. (See Section 4.1.1.). Many of the women appear to have included their right to land back home as ownership. And in four cases out of 89 women, respondents stated that they own a cow. Though we did not get any details about this ownership, it is likely that the ownership, like jewellery is part of the *stree dhan* received at the time of marriage and the right is restricted.

(ii) Productive Assets

Table 3.10 shows ownership of productive assets and suggests that, by and large, the farmer families do not own much farm equipment. This is indicative of the poverty of the majority of the sample households. Nearly 50 per cent of households do not own any farm equipment or other means of production except some hand tools worth a few hundred rupees. About 25 per cent of families reported ownership of one machine/ machine equipment, which could be chara machine (fodder cutting machine that operates manually) or bore/engine for irrigation. About 15 per cent of families own two pieces of equipments and less than ten per cent own three or more pieces of equipment. Eight families reported ownership of tractors—five of them from Agra. It is obvious that most of the farmers are small and marginal with low investment. Mostly families take on rent equipment like a tractor for ploughing and spray machines for application of fertilizers and/or pesticides. These rentals increase their cost of production.

Table 3.10: Ownership of Productive Assets Except Land

Category	*Shahjahanpur*	*Pratapgarh*	*Agra*	*Total*	
				Number	*%*
Nil	31	36	21	88	48.6
Nil or up to one	49	48	39	136	75.1
Nil or up to two	58	55	51	164	90.6
Chara machine	7	13	33	53	29.3
Bore	23	15	21	59	32.6
Engine	9	8	5	22	12.2
Tractor	1	2	5	8	4.4
Thresher	0	3	4	7	3.9
Others	2	1	1	4	2.2

Note: Figures are in numbers.

When the data is examined in terms of the value of productive assets, the picture is much clearer. About 40 per cent of families own assets valued up to 1,000 rupees and 50 per cent worth not more than 2,650 rupees. The asset value of the next ten per cent of households is between 2,650 to 5,000 rupees. The next 15 per cent of families own assets worth 5,000 – 20,000 rupees. The remaing 15 per cent own between 20,000 to 100,000 rupees worth of productive assets. In total, the 181 families put together own approximately rupees 55.4 lakhs

[5.54 millions] worth of productive assets. Only six households reported owning assets worth more than 200,000 rupees.

(i) Household Goods

Five poor households reported that they own nothing worth reporting. The most common asset available is a bicycle, with one in every two families. The other two common household goods are television sets and electric fans, followed by sewing machines and motorcycles. Only one respondent reported ownership of a four-wheeled vehicle. Overall, the sample population is not well endowed in terms of household goods (table 3.11). The data clearly suggests that Shahjahanpur survey participants are perhaps the poorest, as they own the least number of household goods. Agra survey participants own the most household goods. This again highlights the relative poverty of the majority.

Table 3.11: Distribution of Households by Ownership of Household Goods

	Shahjahanpur	*Pratapgarh*	*Agra*	*Number*	*%*
Nothing	3	2	0	5	2.8
Bicycle	56	59	49	164	91
TV	10	17	36	63	34.8
Sewing machine	5	18	10	33	18.2
Fan	2	31	37	70	38.7
Motorcycle	1	6	17	24	13.3
Jeep/Car			1	1	0.6
Almirah	1		7	8	4.4
Fridge		1	3	4	2.2
Sofa	1			1	0.6

(i) Livestock

The Table below provides details about the ownership of livestock among the sample households. About ten per cent of families did not report any type of livestock. The most commonly-owned livestock include milk animals: buffalos, cows and goats. In all, 55 per cent of families reported owning a buffalo. However, in Agra, 83.3 per cent of families reported owning buffaloes. The next most common livestock is a cow. Cows are more common in Pratapgarh than the other areas. Ownership of an ox is also relatively more in Pratapgarh. No households in Agra reported owning an ox. Earlier, we had observed that five owned tractors in Agra. It seems that in Pratapgarh, oxen are used to plough the land.

Table 3.12: Ownership of Livestock

Livestock	*Shahjahanpur*		*Pratapgarh*		*Agra*		*Total*	
Type	*Number*	*%*	*Number*	*%*	*Number*	*%*	*Number*	*%*
Nothing	9	15.0	4	6.6	4	6.7	17	9.4
Buffalo	26	43.3	24	39.3	50	83.3	100	55.2
Cow	22	36.7	30	49.2	14	23.3	66	36.5
Ox	8	13.3	16	26.2	0	0.0	24	13.3
Pandya	23	38.3	6	9.9	30	50.0	59	32.6
Goats	11	18.3	11	18.0	7	11.7	29	16.0
Nil plus one	31	51.7	35	57.4	23	38.3	89	49.2
Nil plus two	50	83.3	57	93.4	52	86.7	159	87.8
	60		**61**		**60**		**181**	

3.4 Housing and Living Standards

Table 3.13: Distribution of Households by Type of House

	Shahjahanpur		*Pratapgarh*		*Agra*		*Total*	
	Number	*%*	*Number*	*%*	*Number*	*%*	*Number*	*%*
Own	59	98.3	61	100	59	98.3	179	98.9
Rent	1	1.7			1	1.7	2	1.1
Kachha	24	40.0	13	21.3	3	5.0	40	22.1
Puckka	11	18.3	19	31.1	38	63.3	68	37.6
Mixed	25	41.7	29	47.5	19	31.7	73	40.3

Table 3.13 gives some indication of housing and living conditions. By and large, everyone owns a house, except two households, one each in Agra and Shahjahanpur. However, housing situation varies considerably across the three districts. About 22 per cent live in *kacha house,* 17 in a temporary structure and another 40 per cent in mixed houses. A sizeable

number of *kacha* houses are in Shahjahanpur (40 per cent of the district). In Agra, just five per cent live in *kacha* houses and in Pratapgarh 21.3 per cent.

Looked at differently, the most *pucca* houses are in Agra, 63.3 per cent. In Pratapgarh and Shahjahanpur, 31.1 and 18.3 per cent houses are *pucca*. The housing situation thus varies considerably across the three districts. This variation is in both type of and size of the houses.

Table 3.14: Distribution of Households by Select Facility in House

Category	*Shahjahanpur*		*Pratapgarh*		*Agra*		*Total*	
	Number	*%*	*Number*	*%*	*Number*	*%*	*Number*	*%*
(a) Separate kitchen facility								
NA	1	1.6	1	1.7	2	1.1		
Yes	9	15.0	44	72.1	11	18.3	64	35.4
No	51	85.0	16	26.2	48	80.0	115	63.5
(b) Separate toilet facility								
NA		1	1.7	1	0.6			
Yes	12	20.0	14	23.0	16	26.7	42	23.2
No	48	80.0	47	77.0	43	71.7	138	76.2
(c) Source of drinking water								
NA	1	1.6	1	1.7	2	1.1		
Tap	41	68.3	20	32.8	50	83.3	111	61.3
Bore	11	18.3	4	6.6	6	10.0	21	11.6
Handp	7	11.7	27	44.3	1	1.7	35	19.3
Other	1	1.7	8	13.1	2	3.3	11	6.1
(d) Electricity facility								
NA	3	5.0	1	1.6	1	1.7	5	2.8
Yes	12	20.0	32	52.5	49	81.7	93	51.4
No	45	74.1	28	45.9	10	16.7	83	46.0
(e) Source of fuel								
NA	1	1.7			2	3.3	3	1.7
Gas	24	40.0	8	13.1	12	20.0	44	24.3
Wood	24	40.0	33	54.1	45	75.0	102	56.4
Gobar	11	18.3	20	32.8	1	1.7	32	17.7

Table 3.14 provides details of select facilities inside a household, including a separate kitchen and toilet, electricity, a source of drinking water and fuel. These facilities help

determine the standard of living. Especially for women, these facilities are extremely critical. The type of kitchen and source of fuel and water are critical in determining their status. The fuel and water source has direct bearing on the women's work burden, as does the use of a toilet. In the absence of a toilet, women suffer more than men.

Most of these facilities are highly inadequate though there is considerable regional variation in household facilities. The table suggests that almost two-thirds of the women surveyed do not have a separate kitchen. Surprisingly, once again, Pratapgarh had the most kitchens (72 per cent of households). On the other hand, only 15 and 18 per cent of survey participants reported separate kitchens in Shahjahanpur and Agra, respectively. There are fewer separate toilets than kitchens. Of the total families, more than three-fourths did not report toilet facilities.

Over 60 per cent reported tap water facilities. Hand-pumps is the second important source of drinking water (about 20 per cent) and bore-wells are the third most common drinking water source (11 per cent). However, there is wide variation in the three districts. In Agra, more than 83 per cent of families have tap water facilites. In contrast, only about 32 per cent of families have reported this facility in Pratapgarh. Overall, about 46 per cent of families do not have electricity in their houses, most likely because they cannot afford an electric connection. During a focus group discussion in Shahjahanpur, for example, many families reported that they are now surrendering electricity connection because of the high cost of electricity. So de-electrification is occurring in the sample villages. Fire wood is the major source of fuel (56.4 per cent). Gas is used in 24.3 per cent of the households. Cow dung is used by the remaining 18 per cent. However, in Agra cow dung is hardly used; the majority use fire wood (75 per cent). Pratapgarh has a very low reported use of gas (13 per cent) and cow-dung is used by almost 33 per cent of the families.

3.5 Summary

In Chapter 2, we had observed on the basis of the secondary data that the overwhelming majority of the farmers are small and marginal. The survey validates that for the sample areas in UP.

The survey findings also corroborate the general poverty of the majority of the farming community, despite the fact that the sample population falls in the command area with a high percentage of irrigation facilities and cash crops. There are several indicators that indicate the socioeconomic backwardness of the sample households.

Agriculture is the main occupation for the majority; 90 per cent have reported owning livestock and the sample households are involved in high value cash crop production of vegetables. Yet, the farm outputs are not sufficient for survival. Families have to resort to wage labour to survive. Almost half the households cannot even afford electricity connection/gas connection. The overall asset base is very low. The majority of the households do not even own agricultural equipments. Half the families do not even own essential household items like fans and television sets. And there is nothing to cheer about living conditions. More than three-fourths use wood and cow dung as fuel. Two third of the women do not enjoy the facility of a separate kitchen. More than three-fourths did not report toilet facilities.

Survey findings also establish the secondary position of women. Assets are owned by males. Only a little over six per cent of women reported land ownership. The extremely low levels of education, and 85 per cent of marriages at less than the legal age reveal the social backwardness of the sample population. The level of education of men is almost three times that of women. The gender difference increases with the level of education: the higher the education, the more the difference.

4

Seclusion of Women: The Means, Process and Implications

Contemporary world history is a history of inequalities and one of the most basic inequities is that between men and women. This inequality has two aspects: biological and socio-historic. And it is the latter, often referred to as gender inequality, that is of concern here. On the basis of field evidences, this chapter attempts to understand the extent, nature, bases, processes and implications of gender differences in the families and communities involved in agriculture-related work.

4.1 Means of Seclusion and Control over Women

Seclusion places physical and social restrictions on women. Women stand denied of several rights: the right to mobility, right to participate in decision-making, right to education and others. It severely restricts the right to choice and opportunity and creates dependency as male mediation becomes necessary for women to interact with the outside world, be it markets, government agencies or banks. Male dependence is an essential outcome of seclusion. It is created and perpetuated through socialization, primarily using means like denial of property rights, *parda*[18] (veil), domestic violence et cetera. This section looks at two basic means of seclusion that enforce and reinforce subjugation of women: the veil and male control over means of production.

As we noted in Chapter 2, ownership of land is crucial in agriculture, as it determines access to credit, inputs and control over incomes and has important bearing on social status. In the present hierarchical society, ownership of land is not only a source of livelihood, but also a source of social and political power within communities as well as within families, especially in rural areas.

4.1.1 *Ownership of Means of Production and Other Assets*

> The absence of claims to property can not only reduce the voice of women, it can also make it harder for women to enter and flourish in commercial, economic and social activities (Sen, 2005, p. 235)

(i) Ownership of Agriculture Land

Table 4.1 gives a broad picture of the ownership pattern of cultivable land within households. A paltry 6.1 per cent of women reported land owned in their name. The district-wide details suggest that in the most developed area of Agra only 3.1 per cent of women owned land. Women owned the highest percentage of land in Shahjahanpur. Interestingly, the percentage of land owned by women is low even in Pratapgarh, where there is more gender equity in agricultural participation and decision-making, (Chapter 5 Sections 5.1. and 5.2) and where the sex ratio favours women (Section 3.1).

Table 4.1 : Ownership of Land by District (per cent)

Owner of Land	*Shahjahanpur*	*Pratapgarh*	*Agra*	*Total*
NR	5.0	1.6	5.0	3.9
Husband	66.7	73.8	73.	71.3
Father		1.6	1.7	1.1
Father-in-law	8.3	9.8	6.7	8.3
Self	8.3	6.6	3.3	6.1
Other	11.7	6.6	10.0	9.4

(ii) Ownership of Residential Houses

Women are responsible for all the household work, but they have no legal right over the house. Women's residential property ownership rights are comparable to their rights over cultivable land—around six per cent (Table 3.11). Ownership by men is over 91 per cent. These men, therefore, enjoy traditional social power to throw women out of the house at any time on charges they may like. Since women do not have a legal right to occupy the property, they are often left stranded despite safety provisions in domestic violence related legislation.

(iii) Ownership of Other Assets

In addition to ownership of land and a residential home, women survey participants were also asked about the ownership of other assets. Almost half the survey participants answered that they own assets. However, a closer look suggests that much of such ownership is notional and not effective. For instance, two-thirds of women's assets related to ownership of jewellery that women received as dowry. However, several survey participants qualified that the nature of ownership, even in the case of jewellery, is restricted to use only. They have no right to dispose of, or gift the jewellery to anyone. The perceived ownership of assets therefore is deceptive.

4.1.2 The Parda System

In the long human history in India, the *parda* system is not actually very old. No record of it exists before the birth of Christ. It likely got introduced during the eleventh century AD. The practice started with the arrival of Muslims in India (Agarwal, 1998). However, within India, it did not permeate uniformly. The south and east Indians and most tribal communities do not observe this practice. However, the mainstreaming of the tribes, especially in north India, introduced the *parda* system among some tribes like the Bhils in south Rajasthan. The most affected area is north India where this practice has been ruthlessly practised. *Parda,* in its wider sense of restrictions and subordination of women, has been in practice for a much longer period in history with wider and deeper influence.

In the study area, we found that the *parda* system has been in practice for quite a while. The survey participants reported that not very long ago—some two generations ago—it was so rigidly followed that women were not allowed to step outside the house and interact with outsiders. Women were not allowed to work in the fields either. The Hindu ethos related to virginity and sanctity was strictly followed. This is reflected in the age of marriage of the survey participants. As we noted in the previous chapter, the majority of survey participants got married before attaining adulthood. A sizeable percentage got married even before attaining the age of puberty (See Section 3.2.3).

In the recent past, however, there have been some changes in this practice and the extent of discrimination has changed.

During the survey, we asked women survey participants about these changes. All women except one noted a change in the *parda* system. The perception about the extent of change is quite varied from a minimum of about 25 per cent to a maximum of 80 per cent. These variations are most likely guided by the life experiences and knowledge of the history of the *parda* system.

The loosening of the *parda* system is directly linked to women's participation in agriculture, as well as their mobility and interactions with other men. Despite this claim of change in the system of veil, we experienced, especially in Agra, that the system is still ruthlessly practised. The depth and strict adherence of the practice was obvious during the focus group discussions in the village Karhara, Agra. The discussion was held on the roof top of a house and no man was present nearby. Yet, there were women who had veiled their faces. When asked as to why they had covered their faces, the following responses were received:

> 'If someone looks here they will go about saying, so and so's daughter-in-law was sitting around showing off her face'
> 'She was showing her nose'
> 'She showed her mouth'
> 'They will tell our husbands and we will be beaten up'
> 'Look how she dances around'
> '*Parda* is practised not only with men but also by young women in front of older women'

In several other focus group discussions, men as well as women were divided on the issue of the *parda* system, and many in both genders said that the *parda* is good, as it maintains respect. Though there is no unanimity, the majority still appear comfortable with the practice, though not in its extreme form, and consider it an important social practice that should not be disbanded (focus group discussions, opinion leaders, Agra). If we examine the above observation in conjunction with other observations related to practices affecting women, we can conclude that even though the *parda* system has changed recently, women are still secluded and the domination of men continues. There are changes but they are too few to make any impact on male domination in the family. This is amply reflected in our study in various ways. The sections on implication of seclusion in general and domestic violence in particular, as discussed later in the chapter, provide more evidences to bring this point home.

Domestic violence is the most common method to ensure subjugation, including the *parda* system. Women in the study reported wife-beating by husbands. Domestic violence is so regular and severe in some cases that one of the women in the group repeatedly asked the facilitator to take her to the city so that she could escape the violence around.

4.1.3 Other Means of Control

(i) Man is Head of the Household by Default

The head of the household known as *Mukhiya* has control of the family. That our social system is male-driven is obvious from the fact that the man is head of the household by default. In our study, out of 181 survey participants, only 14 (6.1 per cent) households reported women as head (Table 4.2) of the household.

Out of these, a majority became the head because their husbands died. So the status of the head of the household was bestowed on them along with widowhood. The other ways by which women become head of the household are long-term migration of the male members or when they are deserted, again in times of exigencies. Women-headed households are thus in fact victims of circumstances and occupy the position not out of choice but under the force of circumstances.

Table 4.2: Type of Head of the Households by District (Per cent)

Type of Head	*Shahjahanpur*	*Pratapgarh*	*Agra*	*Total*
Man	89.8	90.2	95.0	91.7
Widow	5.1	8.2	5.0	6.1
Other	5.1			2.2

Not unexpectedly therefore, even when women become heads of households, they do not perform all the functions and roles that men typically perform as household head. They do not pass their role even on to grown-up and educated girls in the household. Case Study 1 is a classic case of gender ideology that shows the secondary position of women in the society studied. This case indeed reflects a dominant reality.

But social reality is not always linear. Contestation is also a reality. This will be discussed in some detail in Section 4.4.

Case Study 1: It Does Matter if You are Boy

Manju, 20, of village Malpura in district Agra is the eldest of six sisters. Her father, who worked in the army, had left his job seven years ago to get his share of 20 *bighas* of land from his elder brother. The untimely death of her father, when she was in standard nine at school, had forced Manju to take charge of the family. With support from close family, she could pull against the odds and bring a semblance of order in the family.

'But it is my *tauji* who will decide my marriage', says Manju. Not only that, all decisions related to the farm–crop varieties, cultivation practices, labour hiring and marketing–are held by her *tauji*. That she is a graduate and has the necessary experience doesn't matter. 'My mother, as the tradition goes, thinks that marrying girls who don't have a brother isn't easy because most think that the groom will spend the better part of his life taking care of his bride's family,' laments Manju. To get the conditions right, her mother not only legally adopted

Devendra, the eldest son of her *tauji*, but transferred three bighas of land to him as well. The adopted son and his wife share part of the same house but maintain a separate kitchen.

'Being a *panchayat pradhan*, my *tauji* has acquired a social status that empowers him to take unilateral decisions,' recalls Manju, 'refusing to grant me the permission to take up the offer of teaching in a local school.' Whether or not her mother regrets the decision to adopt a son, she is convinced that daughters can't own land. In her life, she hasn't come across a case where daughters are land owners. After all, she had six daughters one after the other, just in the hope of getting a son.

'I was too young to understand the legal rights. I do understand them now but have been socially constrained to not assert myself. My mother is my greatest worry, who will look after her after we sisters get married? Devendra is a "son" only on paper. He neither takes care of my mother nor we sisters have any emotional bonding with him.' Continuing after a pause, Manju said 'I wish I could get a husband who would agree to my taking care of my mother after marriage.'

4.1 The Process of Seclusion

4.2.1 Domestic Violence

We asked women their opinion on seven different common domestic violence practices at both the individual and community level. The results suggest that domestic violence is quite common among surveyed families. The acceptance (by women) of violence at household level is relatively lower than the violence at the community level. It would not be unreasonable, however, to assume for obvious reasons that information at the community level may be to some extent a projection of the household-level reality. The results related below are self-explanatory:

(a) More than 80 per cent of women surveyed agreed that they face scolding from time to time at home. At the community level, it was 89 per cent and stated frequency is often too regular in majority of the cases. In Agra, the responses at household and community levels differ considerably, by almost 20 per cent.

(*b*) Not only scolding, hitting is also common—48 per cent at home and 87 per cent at the community level. This happens not very often though. The discrepancy in the findings relating to home and community is quite substantial in the case of severe beatings/thrashing—eight times from 8.3 per cent to over 64 per cent. This means that women do accept occurrence of violence in the community but refuse to accept that it happens within the household.

(*c*) From a regional perspective, domestic violence appears to be more prevalent in Shahjahanpur than in the other two districts.

(*d*) No respondent said that there has been a case of burning in the house. However, at the level of the community, 18.2 per cent respondents cited cases of women burning. The reporting was highest from Shahjahanpur (30 per cent), followed by Agra (20 per cent) and Pratapgarh (4.9 per cent). However, such cases occur once in a while. The primary reason for this is attributed to dowry. Sometimes, women are burned for other reasons as well, like refusal to have sex, obecting to alcohol consumption, et cetera.

(*e*) The female survey participants also primarily experience the problem of desertion at the community level (30.9 per cent). Pratapgarh women (36 per cent) reported more about this problem compared to the other two districts. The reasons for desertion are similar to the types of violence.

(*f*) Women also articulated that there is a problem of women being killed and/or thrown out of the house at the community level. There are a few cases where it has been articulated at a household level, but mostly women have said that these kinds of violence against women do happen in the community. The number of women who perceive such problems is small (12–18 per cent) for the total sample. Shahjahanpur appears to be a problem area, as about 25 per cent women reported it there.

When inquired, several reasons were given for the violence,

such as food not been offered on time, refusal for sex, arguing, minor mistakes, man get drunk, less dowry, when children are hit by men, unfaithfulness, not paying attention to housework, et cetera. It is obvious that most of these reasons are mere excuses to justify violence. A closer look at the reasons reveals other aspects of family violence: that the women have no control over their bodies; they have no right to refuse sex; there is the practice of dowry in the area and dowry-related violence does take place; women have to be perfect; they have no right to make even small mistakes; they can only be followers and have no right to argue or dissent.

Domestic violence in the sample households is rampant. To put it in other words, the level of subjugation of women is quite high. To avoid violence, women surrender, suffer and avoid any kind of confrontation. This is reflected in the coping strategy that will be discussed later in the chapter. Unfortunately, the violence continues despite the fact that there is a strong law against it. It is likely to continue because both men and women consider it a part of life. Domestic violence, therefore, perpetuates subjugation.

4.2.2 *The Male Control Over Mobility and Choices*

In Chapter 5 we discuss decision-making processes related to agricultural activities. We shall therefore only mention here the fact that decision-making in general is, by and large, a male bastion. This is true not only in agriculture but also in the education of a child, marriage or employment. During the course of the survey, several female participants said that they wanted their daughters to continue with education but their fathers refused and got them married instead. In other instances, fathers refused to send daughters to towns/cities for further education. In the absence of the father, brothers or other male elders exercised this control (see Case Study 1).

4.2.3 *The Traditional Beliefs*

Some discriminatory practices originate in traditional beliefs about girls. The community at large believes that a girl is a liability, and that she is weak and vulnerable, and therefore needs to be confined to the house. Girls are discriminated against from the moment they are born. Arguments are given that restrictions on the girl's mobility are for her own good, and safety. The concern for a girl's safety is nothing more than control over her sexuality. Thus, the beliefs that girls are a liability and require safety are ingrained in the process of socialization and become important rationale to the ongoing processes of subordination.

(i) A Girl is a Liability

In common cultural practice the dowry appears to be one important reason for preference for boys, in addition to the other issues of morality and dislocation after marriage. A girl is considered a liability (Box 4.5). She is not considered part of the family, as she is likely to leave the family after she is married. This belief permeates through the family and community members, in the mother, father, family, community and all others. She is considered a 'property' of someone else that is in the care of her parents. Naturally, therefore, the parents would not like to invest in her and would be extra careful to ensure that nothing 'wrong' happens to her. No wonder, therefore, that even the traditional birth attendants do not expect a gift when a girl child is born. It is this belief system that establishes discrimination against a girl from the moment she is born. This has to be contested for change to occur.

(ii) Women's Place is at Home (and Not in the Market)

Most men think that a women's rightful place is at home and not in the market.

> 'Women's work is within the household, looking after children. All this has to be done by them. There are farm animals, the women have to take care of them. They get involved in housework, looking after animals and children'.
>
> 'If women go to the market who will give food to the men? This is the main reason'.
>
> 'Women cannot do this work in the vegetable market, will they go at night? Which woman will go and work there at night?' (focus group discussion, men, Malpura, Agra).

4.3 Implications of Seclusion

The ideology and practice of seclusion has a devastating effect on human society, as it leads to and sustains the processes of division, oppression and dehumanization. In this section, we will discuss the implications of seclusion on some of the important aspects of women's lives like education, work burden, et cetera.

4.3.1 Differential Education Levels

Table 4.3: Education Level of Male Heads of Household

	Number	%	*CP*
Illiterate	51	30.5	30.5
Up to Class 8	63	37.8	68.3
Class 9-12	42	25.1	93.4
Beyond school	11	6.6	100

Note: CP = Cumulative percentage

The role of education in the present social context need not be overemphasized. It is now universally accepted even by the critics of the present education system that education is important. The practice of seclusion in India has deprived sections of society of this essential human and social need. Historically in Indian society, seclusion has been both societal as well as gendered. Within the caste system, the lower castes were deprived of education and this still continues, but perhaps to a lesser degree. Sex-based seclusion however cuts across communities. Thus, within the secluded communities, women are further secluded. Historically, women have had marginal education levels in the communities in question, a practice that continues in the present as well. But there have been some recent changes. Here, we will explore changes in the education of the girl child.

Table 4.4: Education Level of Female Survey Participants

	Number	%	*CP*
Illiterate	138	76.2	76.2
Up to Class 8	34	18.1	94.4
Class 9-12	7	3.6	98.9
Beyond school	2	1.1	100

If we compare the education-related data of women survey participants with those of men who are head of the households, we find the extent of differences in men and women's education. Seventy-six per cent of women survey participants reported that they never received formal education (Table 4.4). The corresponding figure for male heads of households is only 30.5 per cent (Table 4.3). The level of illiteracy among women is more than two and a half times that of men. The average years of formal education also differ considerably. Out of 181 female survey participants, only seven women reported that they studied beyond the 8th standard and only two received education beyond the 12th grade. On the other hand, out of 167 male heads of the household, about one-third reported having studied beyond the 8th and 11th classes. The ratio of men and women's education between the 8th class and beyond the 8th is 63:53 and 34:9. The educational impact of seclusion on women is very high in the current adult sample population.

The present situation of children may be slightly different, but the educational impact is still markedly different for girls and boys. There have been changes in the education scenario over the past several years. Those surveyed perceived changes in girls' education to be greater than the changes in the *parda* system. 64 per cent reported a change of 60 to 90 per cent in girls' education. The highest change-level was in Pratapgarh where one-fourth reported a change of 90 per cent.

We can really appreciate and understand the perceived changes in girls' education if we look at the education level of the women survey participants noted above. The mothers' level of education has been extremely low. The girls now go to school at a higher rate. This explains the high level of perceived changes in girls' education.

This perception, however, is misplaced in a sense, because even now there is considerable discrimination in girls' education. Girls are sent to the local school only until a certain age. Once they come of age, male control and restriction on mobility continues to be significant. Girls are not sent out of the village, they are forced to help domestically and otherwise. There are ample instances of this in our study. For example, the following quote testifies to this problem:

The boys are better educated because the school is at a distance from the village and because parents do not send girls to school. The other reason for not sending girls to school is that they have to contribute to household work (focus group discussion, adolescent boys, Todarpatti, Pratapgarh).

4.3.2 Sex-based Division of Work

The seclusion of women leads to sex-based division of work. Since seclusion restricts mobility, the women's activities are restricted in and around home, or at the most, the agricultural fields. Because of their low level of education, they do more menial work than men. In Chapter 5 we discuss sex-based division of work in agricultural activities and underline in detail how women are excluded from market- related and skill-based work like handling tractors, electric pumps, engines, et cetera. Socially significant work remains under men's control. The elevated status of men's work is a social construct as any work that has market value or adds to market value is socially significant.

The work division is internalized during the process of socialization to such an extent that it is justified on several counts. This emerged in several focus group discussions with women in different villages. It is worth quoting some of the statements women made in response to a question: Why some work is done only by men and not by women? The responses of different women indicate internalized values of women's place in work.

> 'When there is a man at home why will a woman go?'
>
> 'It is not a woman's work to sell in the market, if there is a man in the house, will his self-esteem not fall, if the woman goes to the market and he stays at home.'
>
> 'It is not women's work.'
>
> 'How will a woman go?'
>
> 'If she goes to the market her husband will be humiliated.'
>
> 'They will throw her out of the house saying...get out are you the one now...'
>
> 'She is dancing around wearing a lehanga (Indian version of skirt)'
>
> 'And you will also be beaten up for it then.'
>
> (focus group discussion, Women, Malpura, Agra)

4.3.3 Silent Suffering

One manifestation of women's secondary social position in society is women's responses when an argument with their husbands takes place. Three-fourths of the women surveyed stated that disputes or tiffs with their husband do sometimes take place (Table 4.5). When asked how they cope with this, they stated that most of the time they keep silent (Table 4.6). Only 15 per cent said that they argue with their husbands or fight back. The other strategy women reported was refusing to eat food. Only one woman said that she refused to cook.

Table 4.5: Relations with Husband (per cent)

Argument/ Tiff take Place	*Shahjahanpur*	*Pratapgarh*	*Agra*	*Total*
NR	3.3	6.6		3.3
Yes	76.7	75.4	71.7	74.6
No	20.0	18.0	28.3	22.1

Table 4.6: Coping Strategy Used by Women (per cent)

Coping Strategy	*Shahjahanpur*	*Pratapgarh*	*Agra*	*Total*
NR	16.7	24.6	30.0	23.8
Keep silent	50.0	54.1	50.0	51.4
Fight	25.0	4.9	15.0	14.9
Do not cook	1.6	0.6		
Do not eat	1.7	14.8	5.0	7.2
Other	6.7	2.2		

Even in extreme anguish, most of the women do not think of ignoring their primary domestic function of cooking and feeding. Women in India typically believe that they have to cook and feed and and that they may be unable to muster the courage to defy social norms.

4.3.4 Double Work Burden

A double or triple work burden on women is a well-studied phenomenon within gender studies. We have noted earlier that women work for around 15 hours a day. The present study further confirms this reality. The women in the study, as a routine, wake up early at around four to six in the morning. The majority (60 per cent) stated that they get up around five. And the majority further reported retiring only after ten at night. Most of the women have a long working day of 16-17 hours. In contrast, men work for less than half that time (Box 4.1).

Box 4.1: Usual Routine of Mother and Father (from a focus group discussion with adolescent boys, Todarpatti, Pratapgarh)

Mother's Daily Routine

'She gets up at around 4-5 in the morning. Thereafter she feeds the livestock, fetches water and prepares food. After cooking, she goes to the field and does all the agricultural-related work like irrigation, cleaning, picketing, et cetera. During noon, she comes back home, cooks food and serves it. Immediately thereafter, she is engaged in household work like cleaning cereals, cleaning utensils, washing clothes, et cetera. In the afternoon again, she is busy tending livestock like giving them feed, cleaning, et cetera. In the evening again, she is busy with cooking food, providing food to children and elders, cleaning utensils, et cetera. Finally, she goes to bed at around 10 o'clock at night' A group of boys unanimously concluded that mothers work for about 17 to 18 hours a day.

Father's Daily Routine

'He gets up between 6-7, goes for a stroll, gets ready to go to the market after leaving instructions for everybody else in the household. Comes back either by noon or around 5 in the evening. After coming back, he sits with other men and gossips. Comes back home at around 7.30–8.30 in the evening, has dinner and goes to sleep'. The group was unanimous that fathers work for about five to six hours a day provided there is agriculture work. Otherwise, they do not work even that much.

During the long, day of work, women get very little free time. Three-fifths of the women survey participants stated that they do not get any free time. And those who reported free time further qualified that they have free time only during the summer when there is no agricultural work. However, there is considerable variation regionally. In Pratapgarh, 72 per cent of families reported free time, whereas in the other two districts about 20-30 per cent reported free time. Pratapgarh, in respect to free time, appears gender-friendly. However, when we probed as to what they did during their free time, the responses were illuminating. Apart from some who said that they rest, others reported doing leftover chores, such as holding discussions on essential matters with family, taking care of children, doing house *putai* [whitewashing], knitting, making patties of cowdung, cleaning grain, making sheets out of the small and waste pieces of clothes *(katran se chadar banana) and* helping others and doing housework. In fact, only about 16 per cent of the women survey participants reported that they rested during this 'free time'. Most of the women do not have time for themselves, for leisure or for entertainment.

The work burden becomes extremely severe in cases where the husband is a drunkard, disabled or sick.

Sickness is quite common in these families and adds considerable work load on the women, whether they are single or married (Case Study 2). A single woman's workload can increase considerably even if she belongs to a relatively well-off household and can afford to hire wage labour (Case Study 3).

Case Study 2: Let the Spirits Soar High

Arvind is a daily wage earner in Shahjahanpur, and has his wife and four children to look after. To supplement his meagre income, he occasionally sells vegetables in the open market after procuring them from the *mandi*. Recently, he planted potatoes on his 2 *bighas* of land. Everything seemed to be in order till he fell ill a couple of months ago. The onus of running the household fell on his wife, Sukhdevi. Her workload increased manifold. From daily chores to tending a patient at home, from feeding children to working in the field, the list of diverse work she performs during the day is back-breaking and exhausting. Rather than give up, she took the challenge in her stride. Taking advice from her ailing husband, she will get the desired work done at the farm with the help of hired labour.

Sukhdevi did what she had not done before—buying inputs, hiring labour, and completing the tasks in the given time. Had her husband not been sick, they would have sown a variety of short-duration crops for the market. This time, however, they had to settle for one, potatoes. After her husband recovered, she succumbed to illness due to overwork and exhaustion. Sukhdevi offers words of wisdom: 'Women should always be prepared to face adversities with courage and conviction.'

Case Study 3: Taking it in Her Stride

Omwati, the *Kotedarani* in Karhara village in Agra, distributing rations under the public distribution system. After the sudden death of her husband, she got his job on compensatory grounds. She not only manages the household, but looks after the shop as well as the farm. Omwati has trained her daughter in bookkeeping and related tasks like helping the villagers with their ration cards. At 40, she is far ahead of other women in the village. Her children, both educated, lend a supporting hand.

However, she had to wade through a world of intimidation, corruption and power hierarchy. Omwati had to face the ire of the *pradhan* for not accepting his demands. For not paying him a monthly token fee, she had to face departmental inquiries. Though she regrets doing it, bribing the officials was the only option for her under the circumstances. Since she is committed to procuring and distributing rations to the legitimate card owners, she has won the favours of the villagers who always speak on her behalf. The *pradhan* has not given up harassing her. Though the battle lines have been drawn up, Omwati is bent upon defeating the enemy with her good work and commitment towards the poor villagers. She will not allow anything to be siphoned off. In addition to the ration shop, she is involved in farming on 4 *bighas* of land. She has been able to manage agriculture on her own, from procurement to production and from harvesting to marketing. *'Hamere char haath pawn hain'* (I have four hands and legs), she responds in response to the question on how she single-handedly manages all the tasks. She herself goes with a tractor to pick up supplies and stays through the night when fields are irrigated. She is not concerned about what people have to say about 'a woman in a man's world'. Much to the dislike of the local powers that be, she does not hesitate to provide sugar and other essential items

> on an event of a wedding in poor households. She is different from other women in the village because she neither caves in easily nor gives up on her efforts.

Women have no respite from the work burden and 60.2 per cent said they have to work even if they are sick.

Similarly, 80 per cent said they have never taken a holiday. The only holidays are when they visit their maternal home. Women's suffering under this work burden is reflected in the narration of their problems. In an open-ended question, we asked women to list three important problems they face. About 31 per cent of the women surveyed said that their main problem is the absence of a helping hand at work. The problem was more severe in Agra and Pratapgarh wherein about 40 per cent women desperately sought a helping hand. For instance the opinion leaders in Agra said that, 'Women work one and a half times more than men.' But simultaneously several men not only justified this work load but also considered it necessary, stating, 'If they do not work they will get moody and irritable.'

4.3.5 Defeatist Attitude

Continuous subjugation, over burden of work, domestic violence leads to internalization of a defeatist attitude, including loss of hope, dependence and pessimism. This personality deformation is one of the important implications of subjugation of women. (See Box 4.2)

Box 4.2: Evidence of Defeatist Attitude

- I am not happy and motivated because I work really hard and yet it does not pay me enough.
- We spend our lives juggling jobs between the house and outside but nothing to fulfil the basic needs. we are always worried about the future.
- We did not achieve anything all our lives, complaining now will not take us anywhere.

(Source: Household Interview Schedule)

Despite facing tremendous problems that threaten their very existence, women reported, as noted below, that they are reconciled to their life situation. This shows that they have lost hope and courage to fight and consider their situation as being destined.

4.3.6 Free Labour

The secondary position of women in society has led to another major social problem wherein the women's work is not considered as work. This is a universal problem validated by the present study. We found that most of the women are involved in agriculture but they work as free family labourers and do not engage in any market transactions. The few that go to the market defy social rules and traditions and face several problems (Case Study 4).

Case Study 4: Not for Women as Yet

Amravati Saroj, 58, lives in the Daipur village in the Pratapgarh district. She is a mother of three. Her eldest son drives a taxi in Mumbai and the second son works at a transport factory in Bareilly. Both eke out a living for themselves.Her youngest son supports her through monthly remittances. Amravati has a long story to tell. Her husband, Algu Saroj, earned no more than Rs. 25 a day by pushing carts. With only 9 *biswa* land, options to sustain the family were indeed limited. She would contribute her bit by getting six quarts of *jowar* a day as a wage labourer on someone else's farm. Back home after the day's grind, she would feed her children. She had liked the idea of growing vegetables by the Maurya community. Algu would not approve of it, as it involved going to the *mandi* and dealing with traders. He dreaded the idea of a woman in a man's world at the *mandi*. Amravati's insistence on vegetable growing was tagged to income enhancement, and this helped her win the argument with her husband.

One day, she set herself off to the *mandi* during the early hours of the day, procured vegetables from the *mandi* at Badshahpur and returned home late after making a decent income by selling it off. In the male-dominated *mandi*, she could find a few women trading vegetables. From negotiating prices to procuring credit, she was at the receiving end of male domination. There are no toilet facilities at the *mandi*. Women have to protect themselves. When someone tried to molest her, she fought back to disgrace the culprit instead. Driving her fears away, Amravati now travels to the *mandi* as far as Pratapgarh, Majheli and Bhupia.

'When will the *mandi* be women-friendly?' Amravati wonders.

The study gathered information on how families decided to use money received after the sale of crops. Only ten per cent of women said that they took part in these decisions. If we look at the figure by region, we find that it is the women in Pratapgarh who have said so. These perhaps are the women who also make decisions about the crops, do market work and in fact, work more as managers. Though women in general work more, as noted in Chapter 5, they have little control over income. Thus, *de facto*, their labour is free labour. Their labour is also free because the land on which they work is owned not by them but by their husbands or some other male family member.

The study found that a few women have control over the products of kitchen gardens and wages under the Mahatma Gandhi National Rural Employment Guarantee Act (MNREGA) in Pratapgarh. However, there are not many such women. But this is one kind of work that they feel proud of because it is based on their own decisions and they have control over the product.

4.3.7 Impact on Health and Nutrition

Women are responsible for the cooking and a separate kitchen would serve a woman's well being. The same is true of toilet facilities. In the absence of a separate toilet facility, women suffer more than men. Women's work burden increases if the water source is far from the home. The distance of the fuel source, too, is critical for women. The location of the fuel source not only helps determine the work burden on women but also has severe health implications. Women spend considerable time gathering firewood and most of the respiratory diseases among rural women are due to the smoky environment they have to work in.

In our study, as noted in Chapter 3, almost two-thirds of the households reported that they do not have separate kitchen, and three-fourths do not have a separate toilet. About two-fifths said that the source of drinking water is either a bore well or hand-pump. Only about one-fourth of the families use women-friendly fuel—cooking gas. The rest all use either firewood or cow dung, both of which are harmful to the eyes and the respiratory system.

Women of Agra and Pratapgarh reported problems related to sickness, lack of toilets and access to water as their current important problems. The problem of sickness was more prominent in Pratapgarh, while in Agra, women mentioned problems of access to toilets and distance of the water source more prominenetly.

A group of women in Agra reported that the problem of access to toilets was aggravated when cultivation switched from wheat to vegetables. The women reported that they can use the fields where wheat is growing but not the ones where vegetables are grown. They added that there are people standing in the fields with sticks to chase them away. And this happens even in the morning (focus group discussion, women, Malpura, Agra). This is a burning issue for most women in the area as there are very few houses that have toilet facilities.

4.4 Future Possibilities

Given the present reality, gender equality is a distant possibility in the near future. Some changes are occurring as are noted at different points in this book, and women may be better off than before, but male domination and restrictions are likely to continue. One reason for the entrenched restriction: it begins at birth. 'When my daughter was born, my mother-in-law didn't speak for two days, but when my son was born, she invited many people and celebrated it,' a woman respondent said. On discrimination between boys and girls, a group of adolescent boys remarked, 'Girls face several restrictions like going out late in the evening, consumption of betel-nut, going to cities to watch films and they have no right to fight or argue with men in house.' (focus group discussion with adolescent boys, Todarpatti, Pratapgarh).

Box 4.3: Select Responses to the Question: How are Sons and Daughters Treated Differently in the Family?

- Girls are not sent out for schooling the but boys are sent out for education.
- Educated girls need more dowry and educated boys bring in more dowry.
- Girls help in household chores and boys support in farm jobs.
- Mostly people do not send girls to schools and they help around the house. Boys are sent out to school and they help in outside work.
- Boys are preferred for jobs outside the house and in the market. Girls are not allowed such jobs or to go out on their own.
- There is no difference in our family, boys work outside and girls do embroidery at home, but all of us earn money. Boys roam around and chat to while away time, but girls are supposed to help around the house, learn to be cultured and respect others.
- In rural areas, boys can go out when they want but it is considered troublesome for girls, lest people should talk behind their backs.
- Boys are allowed to go wherever they want, wear whatever they wish but if girls do not do what is expected of them they are considered uncultured.
- A son is free to go anywhere, he is a boy. A girl is not allowed to wear whatever she wants, she is intelligent but cannot be sent to school, going out is dangerous for girls.
- Nobody cares how a boy is dressed but girls have to remain under covers.
- My daughter wanted to do a bachelor's degree and get a job but her father married her off while the sons were always allowed to go anywhere.
- Saxena's daughter is so good at studies that she may get through the civil services but they do not let her study because they would have to find an equally suitable match for her.
- After feeding my son, I don't care too much, but to my daughter, I teach household chores that will come handy later in life.
- Boys can wear whatever they want but girls have to wear what we want and girls must eat only after everybody else has finished their food.

- We will send our son to a private school so that he can get a good job and improve our lives. Our daughter will continue in public school because even if she manages to get a decent job, that money will not be any good to us.
- Once my daughter cried a lot for a pair of jeans but she wasn't allowed to wear one; however, my son got a pair of jeans for Holi.
- When my son comes back from the fields, he rests but if my daughter wants to rest, we tell her she cannot get that tired doing household chores.

Source: Women Farmers' Interviews

The possibility of qualitative change is remote as evident from the responses of women to direct questions on the treatment of boys and girls in the family (see Box 4.3 and Box 4.4). These statements (translated) have been reproduced verbatim. A reading of the statements clearly indicates that gender discrimination continues to be strong in the sample areas. In the case of unmarried grown-up girls, their mobility continues to be highly restricted. They are not given proper education. Higher education for girls is considered a liability. Girls' role in society is not considered beyond domestic work. Girls are not allowed to go to markets. Girls have to follow a dress code; and so on.

A girl faces discrimination the moment she arrives in the world. In fact, the mother who gives birth faces discrimination too. Upon giving birth to a girl, the mother is sometimes abused, not given proper food, not allowed to take proper rest and made to feel as if she has committed a crime. The family mourns, rather than celebrates, the birth of a girl child. Box 4.3 tells the story of the discrimination girls face upon arrival in the world.

Box 4.4: Select Responses to the Question: What is the Difference between the Birth of a Boy and a Girl in the Family?

- There is a big difference. Boys carry on the families while girls are outsiders.
- The birth of a boy is celebrated, while with girls, nobody is happy for the fear of her dowry.

- A girl and a boy are not equally welcomed in the world, boys are made superior by God himself.
- When a boy is born, the family announces the birth by beating plates, and celebrates by *'kuan poojan'* invites people and give gifts, saris to daughters and sisters. When a girl is born, they only perform 'datthon'.
- When a boy is born, his family distributes sweets, celebrates and invites people but when a girl is born, they sit with heads drooping in their hands and call it a burden of Rs 10 lakhs.
- My husband pompously announced the birth of our son, he invited people over and distributed laddoos but when our daughter was born everything was silent.
- When my daughter was born, my mother-in-law did not speak for two days but when my son was born, she invited many people and celebrated with singing and rituals.
- When a boy is born, plates are beaten and gunshots are fired so that the baby grows up strong and unafraid but nothing is done on a girl's birth so that she always remains suppressed.
- A boy's birth brings happiness, celebrations and respect for the mother but a girl's birth is considered to bring disrespect.
- A boy's birth is celebrated with music bands, chanting from the Ramayana and parties but nothing is done on a girl's birth.
- When a boy is born, they beat thalis so he grows up never getting scared and throw water down the drain to ward off evil spirits but nothing is done for the girl baby.
- When a boy is born, several prayers are offered and rituals performed but not when a girl is born.
- When I gave birth to my daughter, my mother-in-law abused me and did not even call the midwife, she was called for by a neighbour. When you give birth to a boy, you get to heal and rest for 10 days but if it is a girl, you have to get back to work right away.
- People think they get indebted forever when a girl is born but they are happy when a boy is born because boys perpetuate the family name.
- When a boy is born, the midwife is happy in anticipation of getting new clothes or some other reward.
- When a boy is born, people think their son will bring more wealth to the family but when a girl is born they think that they will have to sell the family owned land to get her married.

Source: Women Farmers' Interviews

The statements in the two boxes confirm that in the household, as well as community, gender-discriminatory practices are routinely practised and are deep-rooted in both men and women's psyche. Even today, the gender disparities begin with the birth of a child: the birth of boy is a matter for rejoicing and that of a girl mourned. This gender disparity continues at every stage in the life of a girl. Thus gender inequality through the process of discrimination and seclusion gets perpetuated. The discrimination is so deep-rooted that the differences in mobility between a boy and girl are not considered as differences at all, even by mothers. They are considered given–not amenable to change. In the words of a woman respondent, 'There is no difference in our family, boys work outside and girls do embroidery at home, but all of us earn money.' This type of belief maintains the *status quo*. Unless there are concerted efforts to alter this type of thinking, the possibility of change is not very strong.

The only counter point to this situation, if history is any guide, is contestation. It is through the process of contestation that freedom is earned. Unless gender norms are contested, gender equality may remain a distant dream. We will now examine the nature, extent and content of contestation.

4.5 Contestation

Table 4.7: Satisfaction Level with Current Situation (%)

Problem	*Shahjahanpur*	*Pratapgarh*	*Agra*	*Total*
No Response	0.0	4.9	0.0	1.7
Satisfied	90.0	44.3	20.0	51.4
Not Satisfied	10.0	50.8	80.0	47.0

In any society riddled with inequalities, contestation is as much a reality as is subjugation and oppression. This is no different for women. The content, form and extent of contestation differ due to various reasons. The primary motive of any contestation is change in the unfavourable situation. Dissatisfaction and discontent are the basis for protest. Half the survey participants said that they are not satisfied with their present situation (Table 4.7). The responses, however, differ significantly by region. Shahjahanpur survey participants were satisfied (90 per cent). The level of dissatisfaction was very high in Agra – 80 per cent and only half the survey participants were dissatisfied in Pratapgarh.

This brewing dissatisfaction however does not appear to have been translated in sorce of change; we have not found much evidence that the contestation happens at a community level. However, at individual level, contestation happens in various forms. Box 4.5 provides the summary of some cases especially in Pratapgarh wherein women have been fighting for their rights. The contestation manifests in asserting rights through courts and other public bodies, in finding alternate independent sources of income, in treading on men's territory outside the home and in the markets and so on. These are continuous efforts at the household level, and many stand out as role models and show the way forward towards realizing a better world – more equal and humane.

However, simple protests within the male dominated society may not be very successful. In many cases it was found that women have made desperate efforts for their daughters to pursue education. Says one of the respondents, 'My daughter wanted to do graduation and get a job but her father married her off while her brothers were allowed to roam freely.' Another respondent said, 'Saxena's daughter is so good at studies that she may get through IAS but they don't let her study because they would have to find an equally suitable match for her.'

It is also equally true that determined women got what they wanted through contestation and defying social norms, winning the fear of the community and crossing major barriers. They successfully moved forward creating gender-friendly behaviours at the household level. Some of these contestations are provided in the Box 4.5.

Two cases mentioned here (Case Study 4, Case Study 5) are about women who ventured into the male dominated *mandi* to do business. In both cases, the women defied social norms and invaded the male-dominated terrain. The story of Devki

Bua (Case Study 6) is equally inspiring. These are determined women who through their grit and determination sought gender parity through a silent revolution. It may not matter much in the final analysis whether it is done under compulsion or out of choice. What matters is the effort. The women are the role models and their bravery needs to be highlighted and encouraged for emulation.

Box 4.5 : Faces of Contestation

Select responses in answer to the question: Have you tried to implement your own ideas?

- I carry all rituals and festivals according to my wish. I wanted to educate my two daughters, but the school was too far so they could only continue till the eighth grade. In farming also, I stood against everybody and decided to plant soyabeans·
- I tried to liberate my daughters-in-law. I trained them in farming jobs and take them to markets and fairs.
- I am planning to start carpet weaving and want to set up an 'adda'.
- After my father's death, I struggled to get the land registered in my name.
- After my husband's death, I married his younger brother.
- My husband wanted to terminate my pregnancy with our youngest daughter but I was against abortion and decided to keep her.
- My in-law's family wanted me to observe parda and be at home but at the same time expected me to go to the agricultural land to work. I said that either I will observe full parda (that means not go to the agricultural land either) or not observe it at home too. I don't use purda now.

Source: Household Interviews

Case Study 5: Certain Traditions Last Longer

Unlike her contemporaries in the 1980s, Mukhtari Begum is stoutly built for a woman of her age. People in her village, Badaban, call her *Galli Bua*. She is held in high esteem by communities of all castes and creeds, considered a daughter of the village, as she continued staying in the village of her birth, even after her marriage. During her childhood, Mukhtari recalls, she saw strict adherence to the *parda* system. Married at an early age and within the same village, she was not spared either. Veiled from dawn to dusk, women lost their freedom even when the country attained independence. Only upon the death of her father and husband did she realize that she did not inherit any land. Through her adulthood, she took land on lease to feed the family. Women from the Muslim community rarely worked on land but Mukhtari had no option.

Being a quick learner, she didn't take much time to emulate the practices her father and brothers used in cultivating the land. Not only did she seek information about inputs like seeds and fertilizers, Mukhtari ventured into the male bastion with grit and determination. 'I have even taught my mentally-challenged son everything about farming so that he could do the work that I could not. I would walk ahead and he would follow the plough.' Mukhtari's harvest of tomatoes has been the best ever in the village, in quality and in quantity. In one voice the villagers say the quality of her vegetables is indeed excellent. '*Itto baingan lago ki ped phato rahi.*' (Plants are drooping with loads of brinjals), says a fellow villager. She goes to the market to sell the produce, and is called *bua* (aunt) by everyone in the market. She has yet to face a problem in the market. Though she is one of the few women farmers in the village who has been respected and recognized for what she has stood for, it has not changed her mind on *parda* and about women working on the farms. Her daughters have been confined to the four walls of home and rarely venture out. argues: Mukhtari: 'I was compelled to do what I did but would still consider home to be a woman's only bastion.'

Alternatively, when there is no contest, no struggle, there is no change in the *status quo* and oppressive and dehumanizing conditions continue. The story of Manju and her mother (Case Study 1) falls into this category.

Case Study 6

Devaki was 16 when she gave birth to a daughter. And that became another reason for her in-laws to torment her. Two years later, her husband, who loved her and her daughter very much died in an accident. Everyone in the village ousted her daughter saying that she was a bad omen for the family that caused her father's death. Along with her daughter, she went to her parents' home and started working there as a farm labourer. She toiled all day long but did not get the same wages as the male workers. People mocked at her that she wanted to be treated equally as male labourers. People would call her characterless and a whore.

Devaki was almost tearing her hair in frustration, one day, when she caught her glimpse in the mirror. 'I am beautiful', thought she, 'probably that is the reason people say I can't be equal to a man, and see me with bad eyes'. That one moment she decided something in her heart and went immediately to the city, got her hair cut like a man and bought *'dhoti-kurta'* (a dress that men wear in the village) like men. She started dressing like men and took up the challenge to work in the farm just like other men did. But she did not have any land to show the world what she was capable of. So, she went to the village *'pradhan'*, who gave her 6 *bigha*s of land in sympathy. Devaki was happy that she wouldn't have to work for others any more.

Devaki did everything on her piece of land on her own, including, ploughing, planting, fertilizing, irrigation and buying seeds from the market, et cetera. She learnt to ride a bullock cart and started selling jaggery (*gur*) in the market. Gradually, when she proved that she could do everything on her own just like any other man, people stopped backbiting. With time, people started respecting her and calling her Devaki *bua* (father's sister is called *bua*).

Devaki has left a lasting impression on her fellow villagers. Her courage and daring spirit are a perpetual source of inspiration for other women. 'What does it take for other widowed women in the community to live as confidently as you have?' I asked. 'Just a belief that they can live without men!' was her answer.

5

Participation of Women in Agricultural Activities

> 'Where women are the majority of smallholder farmers, failure to realise their full potential in agriculture is a contributing factor to low growth and food insecurity.' (World Bank, 2008)

This chapter focuses on two important dimensions: labour time use by activities and participation in decision making by the different workers. The study included several questions to gather information on the above two dimensions. The time use data was gathered for eleven different activities on a ten-point scale for four different participants: family male, family female, male wage labourer and female wage labourer. The data collected related to specific crop-the last most important crop raised during the Kharif season. The second set of data relates to perception of women about their involvement in decisions relating to 23 different farm activities.

The study is focused on small and marginal farmers who are involved in subsistence farming that is not necessarily for self-consumption. Target farmers grow vegetables and sell a major part for their earnings. They are involved in several activities and usually do not hire wage labour. All members of the family labour on the farm to produce the crop. Women play a critical role as they are involved in almost all kinds of activities, barring a few like using a tractor for ploughing.

5.1 Allocation of Labour Time

The data indicates the following important aspects of the labor time used by different participants in the research areas:

(a) Use of wage labour is quite low among the sample population. The highest use of wage labour has been reported from the most urbanized and prosperous region of Agra.

(b) There are certain activities like land preparation and sowing, buying inputs and selling crops where family males are the main participants.

(c) There are also households where male-dominated activities are handled dominantly/exclusively by the family female, which debunks the myth that women cannot do this work.

(d) The family female works in otherwise male- dominated activities more in the district of Pratapgarh than the other two districts of Agra and Shahjahanpur.

(e) There are certain activities like weeding and harvesting wherein family females as well as female wage workers are predominantly involved.

(f) On average, women spend more time in agricultural work than men do—the reason for this is simple- women do more work in labor demanding field-based activities like weeding, harvesting, sorting, cleaning et cetera. whereas men work more in market activities, which require relatively much less time.

(g) There is a set of activities wherein men and women both participate more or less equally like harvesting/ vegetable plucking.

5.1.1 *Family Male Dominated Activities*

Out of eleven different activities for which information is available, five are highly male-dominated: land preparation, seed purchase, fertilizer application, pesticide application and sale of the crop in the market. We want to note, it is not because women cannot do these activities that men are doing them but it is so due to socialization and traditions.

The fact that women are not typically involved in marketing was substantiated by a group of women during a focus group discussion. (Box 5.1)

Three in five women respondents reported that family males do 80 to 100 per cent of all the work related to land preparation (mainly ploughing). On the other hand, 51 per cent of women surveyed reported that they do not participate in land preparation at all and another 23 per cent reported participation up to 20 per cent (Table 5.1).

Box 5.1: Market and Women Farmers: Excerpts of an Interaction with Group of Women

When asked whether women are part of the decision on what seeds to buy, one of the survey participants said, 'Women are not asked.'

Another woman argued, 'Women have nothing to do with it (fertilizers, seeds). They (men) bring it, we plant it, when it grows and when it is ready we get to know whether it is hybrid or a local variety. Hybrids are bigger in size.'

Yet another woman felt rather offended and added a counter question in her response, 'Our husbands bring the pesticides, do you expect us to bring it? The men in the house go, the women do not go.' When asked why, replied one, 'Women cannot go.'

Another said, 'When you have men to bring it then what work is it of women?'

Source: Focus group discussions, women, Badavan, Shahjahanpur

Though overall the wage labour use for land preparation is low, whatever reported is also male dominated. About 80 per cent (145 out of 181) of the families reported that no male wage labour was employed for land preparation. The corresponding figure for women is 96 per cent (174 out of 181). Simialry, seven families (3.9 per cent) reported that the entire land preparation work was done by hired wage labour but none reported use of exclusive female wage labour. Over 96 per cent of the survey participants said they have not used female wage labour for this purpose.

Table 5.1: Labour Time Use for Land Preparation by Type of Participant and District (in %)

Category of Worker	*Labour Time Use*	*Shahja-hanpur*	*Pratap-garh*	*Agra*	*Total*
Wage Labour Male	Nil	50	53	42	145
Wage Labour Female	Nil	59	58	57	174
Family Female	Nil	23	36	34	93
	20%	25	7	10	42
Family Male	100%	14	27	20	61
	80%	26	7	6	39

5.1.2 Female Dominated Activities

At the outset, we would like to state that higher caste women do not participate in agricultural work.[19] Most higher caste people do not allow their female family members to go out of the house and work on their farms. Such gender biases among the families belonging to the upper social strata, especially in rural India, are very common. Indeed, it is also true that the girls are more educated in such families and they go out for studies and also do high-end jobs. However, they are not allowed to do menial work, work that is traditionally done by lower castes.

The case of a graduate of an Agra family in our sample population shows these dynamics (Case Study 1). She belongs to an economically affluent family, was allowed to pursue studies in college and studied plant science related to plants. Her household owns good farm land, her mother is head of the family and has also held the post of *pradhan*, and she has no brother. Despite all this, she has not been allowed to participate in any of the farm activities. The mother, after the father's death, adopted the son of a brother-in-law in order to carry on agricultural work. He now handles all the agricultural work. Part of the land has also been transferred in his name.

Moreover, our findings suggest that women are not involved in any such farm-related activity wherein no men are involved. In the section above we noted certain activities wherein *only* men are involved in majority of families. We did not find any such cases with regard to women for the remaining six categories. It would not be out of context here to mention that we have not included in this list certain livestock-related activities like cleaning animals, washing and cleaning the animal sheds, making dung cakes, et cetera which in the majority of cases are done exclusively by women.

This is not to suggest that women are not intensely involved in certain farm activities. Table 5.2 related to harvesting clarifies this point, especially with reference to wage labour use. If we look at the figures in the first row we find that 91 per cent of survey participants said that male wage labor was not hired for harvesting work, the corresponding percentage for women wagers is only 72.4 per cent. This means about 28 per cent of families hired women wagers and nine per cent of families reported hiring men for harvesting work. In relation to family labour too, differences are discernable. Relatively more women are engaged in harvesting, in some families up to 100% .

Table 5.2: Comparative Labour Time Use for Harvesting

Participation in %	*Family Male*		*Family Female*		*Wage Labour Male*		*Wage Labour Female*	
	%	CP	%	CP	%	CP	%	CP
0	15.5	15.5	11.6	11.6	91.2	91.2	72.4	72.4
10	2.2	17.7	1.1	12.7	1.1	92.3	1.1	73.5
20	7.7	25.4	13.8	26.5	0.6	92.8	3.9	77.3
30	9.4	34.8	11.6	38.1	1.1	93.9	2.2	79.6
40	8.3	43.1	16.6	54.7	1.1	95.0	4.4	84.0
50	29.8	72.9	31.5	86.2	3.9	98.9	7.7	91.7
60	13.3	86.2	6.1	92.3	0.6	99.4	4.4	96.1
70	9.9	96.1	3.9	96.1	0.6	100	1.1	97.2
80	2.8	98.9	0.6	96.7				
100	1.1	100	3.3	100			2.8	100

Table 5.3: Comparative Labour Time Use for Weeding

Participation in %	*Family Male* %	CP	*Family Female* %	CP	*Wage Labour Male* %	CP	*Wage Labour Female* %	CP
0	23.2	23.2	9.4	9.4	91.7	91.7	67.4	67.4
10	0.6	23.8	2.2	11.6	0.6	92.3	0.6	68.0
20	16.6	40.3	9.9	21.5	1.7	93.9	1.1	69.1
30	11.0	51.4	11.6	33.1	1.1	95.0	3.9	72.9
40	11.6	63.0	15.5	48.6	1.7	96.7	4.4	77.3
50	14.4	77.3	22.1	70.7	2.8	99.4	12.7	90.1
60	13.3	90.6	10.5	81.2	0.6	100.	5.0	95.0
70	6.1	96.7	7.7	89.0			2.2	97.2
80	2.8	99.4	3.3	92.3			1.7	98.9
100	0.6	100.	7.7	100.			1.1	100.0

Table 5.3 clearly shows that weeding is a female-dominated occupation irrespective of whether it is done by family labour or hired labour. One-third of households reported hiring women wagers for weeding, compared to less than ten per cent of families who hired male wage workers. Similarly, we find that over 23 per cent of families reported that men in the family did not participate in weeding at all. The corresponding figure for women is only 9.4 per cent. As many as 14 survey participants said that the entire weeding work is done by women but in only one did a family man do the entire work. Women are thus more intensely involved in weeding work.

The fact that women are more involved in weeding and harvesting is reflected in other related responses. For instance, one set of questions asked who uses which tools/equipment and for what purpose. It was invariably reported that women use *darati, khurpi* and *hansia* (sickle) and men *fawra* (spade). It was also reported without any exception that tractors, electric pumps and other machinery are operated by men only.

5.1.3 Joint Activities

There is no work which is done exclusively by either men or women, except for handling machinery like tractors. In some work activities, however, men dominated and other activities, involved mostly women. Of the 11 activities, five are male dominated and three are female-dominated. For the rest, like vegetable sorting and packing, participation is more or less alike. There is less gender-based domination in some activities.

5.1.4 Satisfaction Level with Labour Time Use

Satisfaction from any employment is usually linked with expected returns on invested time and other resources. However, in the present case, the expectations may in the first place be relatively less due to their social status, ignorance and repeated experiences of failure. Also, the socialization process teaches women to be contentend and even happy with whatever is available. It is perhaps due to the cumulative impact of all this that, despite the grinding double work burden and loss of crops, the majority of women interviewees said that they are satisfied with the labour time and resource uses. However, one-third of women reported that they were not satisfied (Table 5.4).

Table 5.4: Responses about Satisfaction

	Shahjahanpur	*Pratapgarh*	*Agra*	*Total*
No response	1	2	0	3
Yes	51	36	31	118
No	8	23	28	59
Total	60	61	59	180

In Chapter 4, we noted that women often face violence when they try to reason with their husbands. We also noted adolescent girls are not allowed to raise their voices. In fact, it is considered bad for women to raise their voices or get into an argument.The high level of satisfaction thus appear to be a reflection of a belief system leading to contentment and a culture of silence.

When asked the reason for their satisfaction or dissatisfaction, 17 per cent of women interviewed did not respond, but 41 per cent said that the cause for dissatisfaction was lack of physical strength, because of which they were unable to do as much work as they wanted (Table 5.5). The other reason cited is over burden due to domestic work.

However, on close examination, the two reasons appear as two sides of the same coin. If the phrase 'burdened with domestic work' is a direct expression of the cause of dissatisfaction, 'do not have strength' is an oblique expression of the same term. Women said that if they were not so burdened with domestic work they could participate more in agricultural work. In other words they said that if they had extra physical strength they would have done more work so as to be satisfied.

Table 5.5: Responses about Satisfaction and Reasons thereof by District

Reason for Satisfaction/ Dissatisfaction	*Shahjahanpur*	*Pratapgarh*	*Agra*	*Total*
No response	5	31	13	49
Do not have strength	45	15	16	76
Burdened with domestic work	10	6	30	46
Lack of irrigation	0	1	0	1
Good crop	0	8	0	8
Total	60	61	59	180

Regarding outcomes of the labour and resources used, we inquired about crop production. Most responded that the produce did not meet expectations. In several cases the crop damage was complete. The reasons for damage included excessive rains, soil erosion, plant disease and bad seeds. This highlights the dire state of extension services and the need to strengthen them. This will be discussed in greater detail in Chapter 6.

5.2 Decision-making

Results show that most of the decision-making is male-dominated.

5.2.1 Decisions about Input Use

Decisions about use of inputs like pesticides (Table 5.6), hybrid seeds and fertilizers are mostly made by family males except in Pratapgarh where some women are involved in a few aspects of decision-making. Interestingly, this is despite the the fact that land ownership among women is relatively low (Table 4.1).

Table 5.6: Decisions about Pesticide

	District	*Shahja-hanpur*	*Pratap-garh*	*Agra*	*Total*
Husband	count	50	42	52	144
	per cent	83.3	68.9	86.7	79.6
Self	count	0	6	1	7
	per cent	0.0	9.8	1.7	3.9
Joint	count	10	4	5	19
	per cent	16.7	6.6	8.3	10.5
Other	count	0	3	2	5
	per cent	0.0	4.9	3.3	2.8
Total	count	60	61	60	181
	per cent	100	100	100	100

5.2.2 *Decisions about Marketing*

Decisions regarding marketing are predominantly undertaken by household males (Table 5.7). Pratapgarh is the only exception in this case too where 16.4 per cent of households reported decisions were made by the family female farmers. In the other districts, eight per cent of interviewees reported joint decision-making. It should be noted that in Pratapgarh there are relatively higher levels of participation of women

Table 5.7: Decision about Marketing the Crop

	District	*Shahjah-anpur*	*Pratap-garh*	*Agra*	*Total*
Husband	count	54	42	51	147
	per cent	90.0	68.9	85.0	81.2
Self	count	0	10	0	10
	per cent	0.0	16.4	0.0	5.5
Joint	count	6	5	4	15
	per cent	10.0	8.2	6.7	8.3
Other	count	0	4	5	9
	per cent	0.0	6.6	8.3	5.0
Total	count	60	61	60	181
	per cent	100	100	100	100

because there are more women-headed households. In Chapter 3, we noted that about ten per cent of the families surveyed had female-headed households in Pratapgarh.

5.2.3 Decisions about Weeding

The results shown in Table 5.8 confirm earlier findings that weeding is primarily women's activity. Decisions concerning weeding are made jointly or by the women themselves. It is only in Agra that men are still the primary decision-makers. This may be due to the fact that wage labour is more common in Agra than in the other two districts and decisions to hire wage labourers rest with the men. Thus market linkages dictate that men are the decision-makers even within women-dominated activities like weeding.

Table 5.8: Decisions about Weeding

	District	*Shahja-hanpur*	*Pratap-garh*	*Agra*	*Total*
No Response	count	0	1	0	1
	per cent	0.0	1.6	0.0	0.6
Husband	count	16	4	34	54
	per cent	26.7	6.6	56.7	29.8
Self	count	1	31	1	33
	per cent	1.7	50.8	1.7	18.2
Joint	count	43	25	23	91
	per cent	71.7	41.0	38.3	50.3
Other	count	0	0	2	2
	per cent	0.0	0.0	3.3	1.1
Total	count	60	61	60	181
	per cent	100	100	100	100

5.2.4 Satisfaction from Decision-Making

As Table 5.9 shows, most of the women are quite satisfied with the decision-making process in the households. The level of satisfaction is highest in Shahjahanpur in the range of 88.3 per cent to 98.3 per cent for different agricultural operations and lowest in Pratapgarh, the corresponding range being 54.1 per cent to 95.1 per cent. This is in line with our earlier observations that Pratapgarh is more gender-friendly and Agra the least. Consequently, the voices of dissent are also sharper in Pratapgarh.

Table 5.9: Level of Satisfaction of Women about Decisions

Work Type	*Number/ per cent*	*Shahjahan-pur*	*Pratap-garh*	*Agra*	*Total*
Land Preparation	Number	59	58	59	176
	per cent	98.3	95.1	100	97.8
Crop	Number	57	56	59	172
	per cent	95.0	91.8	100	95.6
Seed	Number	57	50	59	166
	per cent	95.0	82.0	100	92.2
Weeding	Number	60	46	59	165
	per cent	100	75.4	100	91.7
Wage Labour Use	Number	53	41	59	153
	per cent	88.3	67.2	100	85.0
Market Proceeds	Number	55	33	59	147
	per cent	91.7	54.1	100	81.7
Money use	Number	53	36	58	147
	per cent	88.3	59.0	98.3	81.7

A closer look at the table reveals that in Pratapgarh women are quite unhappy that men control the money received from the sale of products (46 per cent) and the expenditures made (41 per cent). They were also unhappy, along with women of Shahjahanpur, with the decisions on hiring wage labor. Given the fact that most women belong to poor families, spending money on wage labour is a potential source of conflict in the family.

We also inquired about why women felt satisfied or dissatisfied with the decision-making process. We did not get many responses but some of the comments made suggest that some women appear resigned to their fate and others are satisfied with participation in decision-making as they feel the decisions are joint. We have discussed in some detail the status of women in the previous chapter and based on that, we may infer that dominant explanation vests in the first aspect. We quote here some of the statements which testify our inference:

'We have to run the house jointly. Men would not take wrong decisions.'
'Men know more, they have seen the world more, they take right decisions.'
'What can I do? I do not know about decisions, it is the job of men.'
Source: Household Interview Schedules.

5.3 Gender-based Division of Farm Work

In addition to the above discussed data on participation and decision making, to understand the perceptions on gender based division of farm work, we gathered information about the work that only men do, that only women do and the work jointly done by both. This information was sought not only form the women farmer respondents but from all the stakeholders.

Here we focus on information gathered about gender based division of farm activities from all the sources put together. The data provide not only the gender based division of work but also provide some interesting facts about the factors that have implications for changes strategies.

5.3.1 Stakeholders Perceived Reality about Farm Activities

In the household interview schedule, we asked directly about gender based divisions of work. This question was asked during focus group discussions as well as during individual interviews like that of the Agriculture Extension Officer. Table 5.11 below provides a summary of responses from different sources about division of farm activities by sex. The table makes it clear that there is certain work that women do not do at all. They relate to use of machines like tractor (ploughing) and marketing, such as buying seeds and selling farm produce in mandis. There are certain activities that are predominantly done my men, like spraying pesticides, irrigating fields, et cetera.

The division of farm-related activities are not necessarily similar in nature at the household level. What is true for one household may not be true for another household. The variations are thus man made and socially constructed.

Table 5.11: Division of Work by Sex

Explanation	*Household–Set 1*	*Household-Set 2*	*FGD*	*Government Officer*
1	2	3	4	[AEO]
Work only men do	• Plowing • Sowing • Transportation	• Ploughing • Apply fertilizers • Spraying of pesticides • Irrigating fields	• Ploughing • 'Mitti chadana' • Spraying pesticide • Bringing seeds • Selling produce • Irrigation • Protecting from Nilgai • Keeping money	• Plowing • Sowing • Irrigation • Threshing • Transporting • Marketing
Work only women do		• Weeding • Harvesting • Sorting • Packing	• Weeding • Tilling • Picking vegetables • Cleaning fields • Planting the saplings • Harvesting wheat • Sorting • Fetching water to mix pesticides	• Storage of hay for farm animals • Weeding • Picking
Work both do	• Weeding • Harvesting • Sorting • Cleaning	• Sowing • Transportation • Irrigation • Putting soil [*mitti chadhana*]	• Weeding • Picking sometimes though it seems to be done by women most of the time.	• Weeding • Picking • Nursery raising

Notes: 1. The household sets are based on several household interview schedules. 2. In household set one there is no work mentioned in 'only women do' category. 3. AEO - Agriculture Extension Officer

Mandi: A Male Bastion that Women Visit Too

Our findings unequivocally suggest that marketing is done by men. Group interviews of brokers and shopkeepers in the wholesale *mandi* (a farmers' market to sell and purchase agricultural produce) suggest that it is primarily a male responsibility. Women, both educated and uneducated, do visit *mandis* but either to buy vegetables or to do manual wage work, not for the purpose of selling the produce. Educated urban women belonging to wealthy families come to buy vegetables for the household. Poor women who come to earn their livelihood, come under force of circumstances. They are either vendors buying in wholesale for onward selling or wage labourers who are usually hired for sorting and cleaning of vegetables.

Since the wage rate is very low, (only Rs. 50), only those who are very poor and do not have alternate work opportunities usually come to work as wage labour. Although the number of women who visit *mandis* is increasing over time, they are currently a very small proportion, about five per cent or so.

In the opinion of the wholesalers and agents, the *mandi* is not a place for women to work. The reasons given included: work is done at night, women's place of work is in the house, market-related work is for men to do and the atmosphere is not conducive for women. To sum it up, in terms of existing social norms, it is not a place for women. Says one agent, 'I have been working here for several years but my daughter and wife do not know where I work. I have never allowed them to come here.' It is for this reason that despite the fact that almost half the shops were allotted in the name of women because of government policy, none of the women have ever come here to do business.

Women who visit *mandis* for livelihood purposes come from distant places and face several problems (Case Study 4). There are no basic facilities like separate toilets. Also women are quite often cheated as they are not familiar with the weighing and bargaining processes. Women wage workers work more but are paid at least 20 per cent less.

The situation is similar to reservation of seats for women in panchayat elections. The women are elected *pradhan* because of reservation of seats for women, but the *de facto* role of *pradhan* is played by male members in the family, be it husband or any other significant male.

It is obvious, therefore, that the laws and policies in themselves are not sufficient to change the social laws under which gender discriminatory practices take place.

5.3.2 Why Women Don't Do What Men Do

The study explored why certain activities are done only by, or predominantly done by, men. Women survey participants were asked why they [women] do not undertake such activities.

Box 5.2 : Select Responses about Women Not Doing Men Dominated Farm Activities

- Most equipment is heavy for females
- People in the village will mock then
- Women are delicate, and men will not like it when women do their jobs
- Women ploughing fields is not socially acceptable
- Women are already overburdened with household chores
- It will be hard for women
- I have done all the jobs, even the predominantly male ones, and have faced many hardships
- Females are never trained for farming in their childhood-Rural women already have lot of responsibilities
- Women are physically weak
- I feel shy
- It's tradition
- Women's clothes like *saris* and *dupattas* are not appropriate for farming jobs, these are prone to get tangled in the equipment
- Men have always done these jobs; if women take over the tractors then men will abandon labouring in the fields

Source: Farm women interviews

Select responses are reproduced in Box 5.2. The statements show that there are two important reasons for women not to undertake men's work: a social barrier, and an already unbearable load of work. Both of these are socially constructed and imposed. Indeed, some women also said that women lack physical strength to handle some of the equipment, so they avoid doing so. However, this was not the dominant reason women gave for not participating in traditionally male-dominated farm work. In fact, some women have even tried to venture into what is typically men's work. The majority of survey participants reported that they do not do so because the community would mock at them, that men would not allow it that they are already overburdened and cannot take any extra work and men already do little and would not do anything at all if women started doing additional work.

One interesting explanation was that women's clothes, consisting of *saris* and *dupattas*, do not allow handling of machinery or doing men's work. The dress code too plays a role in gender based division of work, some women perceived.

5.3.3 Change is Noticeable

In the above section, we noted changes in women's perceptions. However, the social reality is a strong barrier holding women back from greater participation in men's traditional agricultural activities. However, women are making efforts to break in. Men's monopoly in marketing, for instance, is now breaking. Select women are now regularly going to market for buying seeds, fertilizers as well as for selling crops and farm produce. They visit shops as well as mandis in towns and cities. This fact has been reported by all concerned in Pratapgarh. The women visitors are not only widows or from households whose men have migrated to distant places for work, but also those who want to earn more to meet household expenses. Women's participation is not restricted to the markets but is present in all other activities, except for using the tractor and plough. For instance, one NGO worker said, 'Except for driving tractors and ploughing, women do all the work in agriculture. This is an established tradition so women donot attempt to do heavy work (IDI, NGO, Pratapgarh).' Quotes from some of the other survey participants are below.

> 'Two-three women go to Durgaganj market to buy seeds and fertilizers. Six-seven women go to Rani Ganj, Powerhouse and Durgaganj to sell vegetables. They go to earn and meet household expenses.' (Focus group discussion, opinion leaders, Hussainpur, Pratapgarh)

> 'Smt Rajani Patel of village Durgaganjs visits shops to buy seeds and pesticides. She is knowledgeable about vegetable crops. Also, the wife of Shri Amarnath of Jairampura comes here to buy seeds of tomatoes, brinjals, cabbages and chillies. She knows how many fertilizers to use because she applies fertilizers and her husband does work related to pesticides and sells vegetables in the market.' (IDI, Shopkeeper, Pratapgarh)

> 'Women's participation has improved over the years. Earlier they used to come only to clean the premises but now they come for grading, sorting and packaging.' (IDI, Mandi Agent, Pratapgarh)

That women are feeling uncomfortable with such male domination and are keen to permeate male roles is aptly reflected in the following responses of women farmers:

We do not get a chance. Given a chance, we can also do most of the work. However, the spray machine, because of its weight may be difficult to operate.

Similar statements have been made by several others, individually, as well as in groups.

5.4 Summary

The discussions above validate several earlier findings and suggest that there are activities that men do more and there are activities that are women centric. But most activities, both women and men do. However, women's activities are by and large related to the farm level only, whereas men are overwhelmingly involved in many different aspects of work outside. There are threads of integration but these are limited to certain areas and are quite thin. The integration is found in relatively less developed areas.

The increasing level of participation for women in the agriculture activities is not without cost. Several women feel an extra burden of work as the agriculture work is added on to domestic work and their work related to livestock.

So far as the participation in decision-making and market work is concerned, the situation is less rosy compared to the farm activities. Participation of women in management is quite low compared to participation in other activities. This is due to women holding a secondary position with respect to men. The prominent reason for this situation appears to be socio-historic. Historically, women are confined to their homes and are therefore not used to market-oriented work. The situation however is changing. Women are making determined efforts to break the grass ceiling. It is an uphill struggle though.

6

The State and Women Farmers

The role of the State is important in determining the status of women. The State, through its various policies, programmes, rules and regulations, shapes social relations and economic activities. State interventions impact not only broad social relations, including economic activities, but also intra-household relations and the social status of various actors.

During the survey, information was gathered regarding various state interventions, their implementation, impact and road blocks. The information collected related to laws, schemes and programmes (henceforth referred to collectively as 'programmes') about domestic violence, ownership of means of production, education and training, food security, employment and social security. All these programmes have bearing on the lives and status of women in general and farm women in particular. A list of select laws and programmes is provided in Annexure C.

This chapter is divided into three sections. Section 1 discusses the implementation of these programmes and the problems encountered in effective implementation, the implications of non-implementation and the role of the state. Section 2 briefly states the various suggestions that emerged during the course of discussions and, finally, Section 3 summarizes the main findings.

6.1 Awareness, Implementation and Implications

6.1.1 Awareness is the First Step

Awareness is the first step towards effective implementation of State-sponsored programmes. Given the enormity of the problems and strong grip of vested interests over the system, it is unlikely that effective and meaningful implementation of government interventions is possible without awareness among beneficiaries. An effective demand from below is a prerequisite for delivery. We will therefore first examine the spread and depth of awareness about government programmes.

Awareness is Low and Inadequate

Our study finds that overall awareness about the laws that might benefit the surveyed population, as well as the schemes, is very low. Even in cases where people are aware, their knowledge about criteria for entitlement, nature and processing relating to benefits is at a minimum level and inadequate. For instance, during a discussion with the villagers in one of the villages in Shahjahanpur, we found that awareness about MNREGA was not enumerated in terms of 'right'. Villagers hardly knew that applications have to be given for seeking employment. Similarly, awareness that public distribution system shops should open five days a week, and the extent of entitlements the system can provide, was not widely known. Also, people were not aware that a person can apply for a ration card at any time.

By the government's own account, the general level of awareness about important programmes like crop insurance is low across all-India level as well as in the state of UP. A UP official observes:

> At all India level only 4 per cent of farm households had ever insured their crops and 57 per cent did not know that crops could be insured. However, in UP only 1.2 per cent of farm households had ever insured their crops and 56 per cent were unaware that crops could be insured. These data clearly highlight that extension activities in the state need to be revamped. (Kumar, 2005)

During our study, the respondents reported awareness about 16 programmes/schemes/acts (Box 6.1). The information about programs was gatherd thrugh open ended questions in the household questionnaire as well as focus group discussions. The overall awareness appears to be rather weak especially regarding the agriculture-related programs and schemes like subsidized fertilizer, *kisan* cards, schemes related to horticulture, dairy, poultry, seeds, irrigation like drip irrigation and so on.

BOX 6.1: Awareness About Programs/Schemes/Acts

1. Domestic violence; 2. Sex determination (PNDT); 3. MNREGA; 4. A Woman's right in ancestral and father's property; 5. Rebate in stamp duty if land is registered in woman's name; 6. Indira Awas Yojan; 7. Mid-day Meal 8. Scholarship for girls; 9. Janani SurakshaYojamna; 10. Vaccination for farm animals 11. Soil testing, fertilizers for reclaiming waste land; 12. Mahamaya Yojana-Scholarships and cycles for girls having completed high school education; 13. Anganwadi (ICDS); 14. Polio vaccination; 15. Ration card (PDS); 16. Widow pension

Source: Household Interviews and FGDs

However, what is heartening to note is that there was some level of awareness about existence of three gender- specific laws related to prevention of domestic violence, share in inherited property and sex determination.

6.1.2 Status of Some of the Select Schemes/Programs

In this section we discuss the status of select programmes and schemes in terms of awareness, implementation and implications, based on our survey findings.

(i) Agricultural Extension Services

> No one comes here to give any information on farming. The authorities sit in the block office and write down their statistics.
>
> *Source*: Focus group discussion, opinion leaders, Agra

Extension services play a crucial role in realizing the potential of human efforts. It helps apply scientific knowledge in real life situations. The positive contribution of extension services is well known and well recognized, says the AEO, Shahjahanpur.

The first thing is that women need to be educated and imparted technical know-how and this will change the situation. Like we have women drivers of cars and buses, we can teach women to drive tractors. Even if the mindset has to be changed, it will happen over time. Eearlier, there were no women who participated in training: now in every programme there are at least a few women.

Despite the need and importance of extension services, awareness and reach at the ground level are limited and gender biased. The limited reach and bias has been observed in the national survey. According to the NSSO (2004), access to an extension service worker as a source of information for modern agriculture has been extremely limited and biased in favour of large farmers. In UP, for instance, the access was 0.8 per cent for marginal farmers and 3.1 per cent for mid-large farmers. The large farmers had four times greater access compared to marginal farmers.

The state of UP in particular has struggled to provide access of extension services to agricultural workers. The same NSSO source suggests that the access in Gujarat was 16.9 and 27.4 per cent for small/marginal and large farmers. In Tamil Nadu, the respective percentages were 12.2 and 17.8 per cent.

In India extension services are provided under Krishi Vigyan Kendra, a government-implemented and managed network. In each district there is one KVK which acts as a nodal agency for agricultural development. Training and education are important functions of these KVKs. The importance as well as limitation of these KVKs is revealed in the interview of the AEO of Agra (Box 6.2). The interview highlights that (a) coverage is limited, (b) scope of work is wide, (c) there are programmes including special programmes for women farmers, but (d) there is an inherent gender bias. The scale bias is obvious from the fact that none of the women interviewed from Agra knew about the KVK.

The limited access and gender biases in extension services in the research area are obvious in the description of training work as narrated by the AEO Shahjahanpur as well.

There are eight of them who go to provide training. Two of these are women: one a home scientist and the other a plant protection scientist. One provides training on making jams, sauces, et cetera and the other provides training on how to spray pesticides.

The number of extension agents is extremely small in relation to the number of farmers to be covered across the targeted area. KVKs are currently training women to make jams, sauces, pickles. These activities are not only stereotypical but also meaningless given the social barriers women face in the market. Without linking this kind of value added production with markets, it is simply a wasted effort.

BOX 6.2: Interview with AEO, Agra about Functions of KVK

He is working in KVK since 1982 and is involved in coordination and monitoring of KVK activities and programmes.

The main function of the KVK includes: a) On farm trials and research, b) Front line demonstrations, c) Extension functions – training of other service personnel from other departments like Agriculture Department, d) Vocational training for farmers, e) Extension activities like the farmers' fair.

The important programmes/schemes for farmers include: on farm trials, farmers' training, exposure visits, demonstration and farmers' fair at the block level, implementation of the ATMA (Agriculture Technological Mission Authority) programmes for the benefit of farmers(this covers fisheries, dairy, agriculture, horticulture, plant production and veterinary services).

The special programmes/schemes for women farmers are: backyard poultry, dairy, nutritional kitchen garden, vocational training on fruit preservation, embroidery, knitting et cetera. On December 4th, they organize programmes as part of Women Farmers' Day.

The work area includes the whole of Agra District, in 15 blocks. However, they have a few selected blocks. These are, Fatehpur Sikri, Akola, Bichpur, Jagnev, Saiyan where they have ongoing work. There are no women farm managers in this area. Last year 214 training programmes (including demonstrations) were organised on various issues. These were attended by 2993 farmers. The exact number of women participants is not available though most of the trainings have a few women as participants.

28 Courses especially for women were organized which were attended by 294 women. These covered a range of courses from pickle, jam making and sewing to farm-related training.

There are no programmes for couples. However, they are building a guest house so men and women can be accommodated together for trainings.

Table 6.1: Awareness about Agriculture Extension Institutions/ Workers (per cent)

	Shahjahanpur	*Pratapgarh*	*Agra*	*Total*
No response		1.6		0.6
Yes		37.7	10.0	16.0
No	100.0	60.7	90.0	83.4

Our household survey findings further suggest that the majority of female farmers are not aware of available extension services and agents. Only 16 per cent reported awareness. The reason for high awareness in Pratapgarh, could be the presence of an NGO in the area for the last several years.

Table 6.2: Training Experience Beneficial

	Shahjahanpur	*Pratapgarh*	*Agra*	*Total*
No response	0	1.6	0	0.6
Yes	0	21.3	10.0	10.5
No	100.0	77.0	90.0	89.0

The data further suggests that awareness is strongly related with perceived benefits. When asked if KVK-led trainings were beneficial, none of the interviewees in Shahjahanpur replied in the affirmative (Table 6.2). The lack of awareness, therefore, would not generate demand for training. The importance of awareness is thus crucial.

Our study data regarding use of modern inputs further emphasizes the need for extension services and that the reach of current extension services in the study area is negligible. Modern inputs like chemical fertilizers, hybrid seeds and pesticides are almost universally used in the research area (Table 6.3). With regard to information sources on modern inputs, the majority said that they found information through the market, friends or relatives. The role of the government and even NGOs in dissemination about scientific practices is negligible. Those who did not report use of these inputs, stated a lack of awareness.

Table 6.3: Extent of Use of Modern Inputs by Districts (%)

Input	*Shahjahanpur*	*Pratapgarh*	*Agra*	*Total*
Hybrid seed	95.0	95.1	100.0	96.7
Ch Fertilizer	98.3	95.1	100.0	97.8
Pesticide	90.0	70.5	100.0	86.7

Because of lack of authentic information, training and education, there is an adverse impact on the agricultural production, and consequently, on the households. In the survey, loss of production had been reported by several survey participants. There are several different ways in which farmers lose production due to lack of information, which reflects failure of extension services.

Firstly, farmers lose production because of poor decisions owing to lack of proper training and knowledge. Even otherwise, good farmers resort to such practices like use of fertilizers without soil testing—this affects land productivity adversely; applying pesticides against advice; using seed multiple times and wasting water in irrigation. These all affect the production and productivity adversely. Since there is an impact on soil quality, the impact is often long term. There are thus ecological issues as well. The practices lead to unsustainable farming. One of the shopkeepers selling inputs, remarked:

> Farmers do face problems when (a) there is not enough moisture in the soil at the time of sowing, (b) when fields are not irrigated

> on time, (c) when vegetable seeds are sown deeper than required (d) when pesticides are not applied in time, (e) when seeds/pesticides are not genuine/are spurious.

Secondly, the lack of education and training promotes unethical practices by traders and companies. Because of the lack of information, small farmers are completely dependent on the market as the source of information, and often become victims of misinformation, black marketing in fertilizers, greed of traders and false promises of companies. The Agra AEO says:

> There is DAP available at subsidized rates of Rs 500. However, it is available in the black market from around Rs 800 to 1000/kg. Agra is being sent more fertilizer than is demanded, however, there is always a shortage of DAP and no one know where it goes.
>
> Hindustan Lever asked farmers to grow chickory and some other plants which are not used locally, however, due to poor quality Hindustan Lever refused to buy it and these had to be sold in the market at a loss for just Rs 2 per kg.

There are several seeds that are sold in the market. However, none of them are tested, putting the farmer at risk. For example, there are seeds advertising 48 per cent oil in mustard, however, it is not possible, as mostly it is around 40 per cent.

During the focus group discussions, several participants reported having been cheated by the traders and companies. To quote one participant, 'There are times when the shop keeper gives bad seeds and the farmer is, *hath peet ko reh jato* (left empty handed). There was a company that distributed towels and umbrellas along with seeds, duping farmers in the process.' Another participant says, 'I cultivated tomatoes on two *bhigas* of land, the plant grew big but had no tomatoes. When I bought the seeds the trader had praised them so much and 10 grams of seeds costed me Rs. 350. (Focus group discussions, opinion leaders, Agra). Several times there have been arguments between sellers and buyers (Box 6.3). Spurious seeds are one of the major problems.

BOX 6.3: Fight Over Spurious Seeds to Recover Costs but to No Avail

I got hybrid seeds of *bhindi* (okra) from Sadhu Surendar Singh's shop in Abdul Nagar. The plants grew really well but it produced *bhindi* that would turn yellow. I made complaints and even called up the company at Jalna. Cost of a phone call to Jalna was about Rs 400 which I somehow managed. They sent a person who visited my fields with the shopkeeper. During discussions, there were heated arguments and exchange of words. I kept calling him for four days. For three days he had been lazing around in a hotel in Agra. So when he came I was angry and wanted to throw him into the well and flatten his car tyres. The boys in the village got ready to beat him up but he pleaded guilty. So I told him to write in front of me, 'write or else I will not let you go.' Once I said this and made him stand in my field, he promised to refund the costs of seeds to everyone in the area. In the end, the shopkeeper made a huge profit because all the seeds from this company were made free. He became a *lakhpati, crorepati* (millionaire), but no one else received anything. (As told by a farmer in Shahjahanpur)

Thirdly, lack of information from authentic sources denies the farmers the access to markets putting them in a position of disadvantage. They are not aware which market would fetch them the best prices.

Fourthly, the cost of cultivation increases due to modern inputs and simultaneously the risk also increases because of uncertainty of markets.

(ii) Ration Cards

Most families have ration cards. In Shahjahanpur 40 per cent reported that they didnot have ration cards. However, the percentage below the poverty line (BPL) and Antyodaya Anna Yojan (AAY) cards are very low. Given the fact that most of the families belong to lower income groups, low percentage of BPL and AAY cards indicate leakages in the system. Improper distribution of cards came out prominently in one of the group discussions in a Shahjahanpur village. Those in the discussion cited instances of rich families having a BPL card and no poor families. Selection as BPL family depends upon one's relations with the pradhan and capacity to manipulate.20 With regard to ration cards, the women of Badavan villages said: 'The *pradhan* has a card.' With regard to their own cards, they said despite efforts we have not got one and shared various difficulties in accessing this scheme (Focus group discussions, women, Badavan):

> I don't have any card. They listed the names but do not make the card. First they came and told us that this card will be made for you, collected the names but did nothing. They do not give us anything, what can we do?
>
> We spent money on this, they asked for 10 rupees, 20 rupees. We paid it but they did not make anything.

The irregularities in the public distribution system affect the women most as they have to manage the kitchen and provide food to their families. As a result, it is not surprising that the NCW in its draft agricultural policy for women farmers has specifically recommended that the PDS system be made universal. Also, the Government of India has accepted in principle that all the ration cards should be in the name of women instead of men.[21] Section 19 of Food Security Bill 2013 placed in Parliament has this provision.

(iii) Employment Scheme: Job Cards

Table 6.4: Ownership of Job Cards (per cent)

	Shahjahanpur	*Pratapgarh*	*Agra*	*Total*
Yes	26.7	39.3	16.7	27.6
No	73.3	60.7	80.0	71.3
NR	0	0	3.3	1.1

We have noted in Chapter 3 that wage labour households are present across all three target regions. However, only 27 per cent of survey participants reported that they have a job card (Table 6.4). One of the reasons for low interest in employment under MNREGA probability relates to leakages and corruption leading to fake demand and low payment, late payments, and at places, no payment. The other plausible explanation could be lack of awareness of the right to ask for a job and get one within 15 days in the village.

It was clear from focus group discussions that there is deep-rooted corruption in the scheme. To quote:

> There is need for reform in the programme. Despite the fact that money goes into the bank, after entry in muster roll, the village *pradhan* charges Rs 200-300 (per muster roll) per person. Unless these extra demands are met, the wages are not credited in the bank. The method of payment should be set right."(focus group discussion, men, Hussainpur)
>
> MNREGA work is very useful as it provides employment and money when there is no agricultural work. There are several problems in getting the benefit of schemes: (a) there is lack of awareness, (b) the benefit depends on relations with the *pradhan*. He is the sole authority and that is the reasons we have not got benefits. (focus group discussions, women, Todarpatti)

Several similar statements have been made by the participants of different focus group discussions.

(iv) Kisan Cards

Table 6.5: Ownership of Kisan Cards (per cent)

Ownership Type	*Shahjahanpur*	*Pratapgarh*	*Agra*	*Total*
NR	0	0	1.7	0.6
Yes	55	75.4	71.7	67.4
No	45	24.6	26.7	32.0

Despite the fact that the majority of households are farmers who own land and they are also in need of credit, the access to Kisan Cards is not universal. Only two-third families have reported owning a Kisan Card. In Shahjahanpur, the percentage is lowest of the districts studied at 55. However, use of cards appears to be negligible, as most of the families reported that they have not taken out any loans in the current year. Most of the cards are owned by men because the land is typically in their name. The cards are not issued in joint names.

Getting a Kisan Card is not an easy task as is explained by a group of men farmers during a group discussion in one of the villages in Pratapgarh:

> The biggest problem is that the bank manager makes us run around a lot and also demands 10 per cent commission and that too in cash. This is very difficult for us. This is the reason that several needy farmers donot have credit cards. Many farmers have been to the bank for the cards but could not get them made.

(v) The Prohibition of Child Marriage Act, 2006

As we noted in Chapter 4, three-fourths of women get married before they are of legal age for marriage. This law was enacted before Independence and therefore all the marriages reported in post-independent India have happened in violation of this law. It is obvious that the law is grossly violated. This has serious implications for women and their situation.

(vi) Mid-Day Meal (MDM)[22]

The status of implementation of MDM is best captured in the following responses of a group of women (Focus group discussion, women, Badavan, Shahjahanpur)

> Food is cooked in the school but children are given very little food. When children come home crying, you can say that they did not receive food.
>
> Vegetables come to the school but these are not given to the children.
>
> If food is made for 10 days there are 10 days when food is not made. The food should be of good quality.

Dalit women are not employed for cooking as children do not accept food from lower castes. As a result, these women are not given employment.

6.1.3 The Role of State: Primary Issue in Implementation?

The State, through its various programmes, gives the impression that it really cares about the poor and marginal including the small and marginal farmers. However, government programmes are in fact promoting a process of development that generates and perpetuates poverty, hunger and marginalization. In the context of agriculture security of poor farmers, the deceptive role of the State becomes obvious when we examine its role in relation to seeds. During the 'Green Revolution' the State promoted hybrid seeds which were made available to farmers at a reasonable cost without any intellectual property rights. That was a pro-farmer seed policy. In the current phase of agricultural development the state promotes the private sector in the seed market. The structural changes in the seed sector are reflected in the following evidence:

In a state like Haryana, the structural composition of the seed sector has witnessed significant changes since the formation of WTO in 1995–1996. The government and cooperative sector contribution in the total certified seeds of cereals in Haryana State was 77 per cent and 5.62 per cent respectively, in 1990–1991, and both the sectors maintained consistent contribution up to 1995–1996. But their share in the total cereals certified diminished rapidly after the establishment of WTO in 1995–1996 and fell to 34.62 per cent and 4.18 per cent in the year 1999–2000. The contribution of the private sector in total cereals certified seeds was 17.07 per cent in 1990–1991, but its contribution in total cereals certified increased rapidly after the establishment of WTO and reached up to 61.20 per cent in the year 1999–2000. (Kumar, et al 2002)

The story of implementation of the various welfare programmes of the state is no different. The nature and extent of entitlements, the process of implementation, the lack of effective monitoring, structural weaknesses in the schemes and laws all show the deceptive role of the state. Several welfare programmes were initiated immediately after Independence. Over the years, there have been several new and better programmes for the welfare of the rural workers including farmers. However effective implementation remains a major issue.

> Compared to earlier times, there has been extensive change for good in recent times in the programmes. Programmes like MNREGA, IAY, JSY, ICDS, MDM are good programmes. However, they are not properly implemented. (Focus group discussions, women, Toderpatti, Pratapgarh)

Effective implementation of laws, schemes and programmes can change the face of social reality. But experience suggests that the implementation of these laws and programmes, for the rural poor in particular, is extremely problematic. There are several common issues that interfere with effective implementation.

The primary reason for the non-implementation is lack of effective information. Awareness about the programmes is very low. Moreover, individuals often cannot beat the systemic hurdles and social action in the area is almost negligible. Secondly, besides the lack of awareness, there are other issues relating to the very structure of the programmes. The extent of the problem greatly exceeds the reach and provisions of the programme. Thirdly, there is no framework for a step-by-step tackling of the problem. Fourthly, accountability mechanisms are not an inherent part of the programme. All these issues are well known yet the problem remains.

The deceptive role of the State is obvious from the disparity between the promises and ground reality in the context of women's empowerment. In 2001, the Government of India came out with a National Policy for the Empowerment of Women. With regard to women in agriculture the policy categorically stated that:

> In view of the critical role of women in the agriculture and allied sectors, as producers, concentrated efforts will be made to ensure that benefits of training, extension and various programmes will reach them in proportion to their numbers. The programmes for training women in soil conservation, social forestry, dairy development and other occupations allied to agriculture like horticulture, livestock including small animal husbandry, poultry, fisheries, et cetera will be expanded to benefit women workers in the agriculture sector (GOI, 2001, para 5.5).

The actual situation, as reflected in our data, makes it obvious that in the last ten years, the reach has been negligible.

6.2. Suggestions for Effective Implementation

There should be honesty in payment of NREGA; Asha should organize meetings in time; there should be no commission in JSY

> in payment made to women on institutional delivery; selection of Asha should be honestly done. (Focus group discussions, women, Todarpatti, Pratapgarh)

Several action points emerge based on the above analysis. Some of the suggestions emerged directly from the survey participants. A more detailed plan of action will be discussed in Chapter 7. These suggestions are not necessarily new. However, they need reiteration and sincere efforts towards implementation. Without these measures it is unlikely that the intended benefits of various programmes would ever reach the needy.

(i) Effective Awareness, Accountability and Monitoring System

There is a generalized problem of corruption in the implementation of programmes. A system to provide holistic information about government interventions on a sustainable basis is needed. Simultaneously, a mechanism also needs to be developed to effectively tackle the issue of corruption and leakages. Easy registration of complaints, quick action and disposal of complaints and deterrent punishment to the guilty are essential for effective implementation.

(ii) Universal Application

Some of the essential programmes like PDS have restricted access. Such programmes need to be universalized as targeting leads to corruption. In fact there have been several studies suggesting that targeting always leads to biased selections and leakages.

(iii) Gender Sensitive Steps for Market Place

There were several insightful suggestions to make mandis gender-friendly: (a) women and men should get equal wages, (b) women should be made aware of the weight of the produce, (c) they should get competitive rates of their produce, (d) there should be a woman helper in the *mandi* who can help women in weighing and negotiating rates, (e) there should be separate toilet facilities in the *mandi*, (f) there should be a storage area where produce can be kept if it is not sold completely on the same day.

6.3 Summary

Our findings related to extension services suggest that none of the farm women have ever benefited from the existing extension services of the government. The reach of extension services to marginal and small farmers appears to be negligible. Presently, the extension services also tend to be not only male-biased but also scale-biased.

There is a low level of awareness about laws as well as programmes. There is no public pressure from below for effective implementation.

Men and women both find the programmes quite useful.

However, simultaneously they also find it difficult to benefit from them because of high levels of leakages and corruption. Such corruption has been noted not only for schemes where the access is restricted, but also for legal universal entitlements like employment under MNREGA.

There are several structural reasons as well that render programmes ineffective when it comes to implementation. The important ones include restricted access, lack of accountability and monitoring, gender biases, et cetera.

In totality it appears that the state is deliberately deceptive in its implementation of pro-poor programms.

7

Summary of Findings and Recommendations

This chapter is divided into three sections. Section 1 summarizes the main findings of the study. Section 2 outlines various constraints and opportunities identified during the course of the study. Finally, Section 3 describes possible interventions at different levels by different stakeholders. The suggestions include both general as well specific within overall strategy of qualitative changes as.

7.1 Summary of Findings

The study results identified the following problems: (i) the various government programmes hardly benefit poor, small and marginal farmers and agricultural extension services are non-existent and require reorganization; (ii) gender relations continue to be very unfavourable to women, the beliefs, attitudes and behaviours, across age, gender and community, continue to be heavily loaded against girls and women; (iii) the contestation process is very weak despite awareness about gender-friendly laws.

7.1.1 Participation of Women in Agricultural Activities

The findings suggest that though women are involved in fewer activities they spend more time on them and are considered to be engaged in 'less significant' work.

Women participate in other activities that are home-based and are perceived to be of lower value like cooking, cleaning animals, making dung cakes, weeding, harvesting, hoeing, et cetera. The division of work is perceived to be due to the nature of work itself. Men do work that involve a lot of hard physical labour like ploughing. The gendered division of work is related to dominant social beliefs and attitudes. The women are confined to homes, away from market-oriented work.

There is gender division of tools as well. Women's tools include, *hansia, khurpi* and *datia*. Men's tools include spades and other machinery like tractors, threshers, et cetera.

In general skill based work and work related to market linkages and those involving financial transactions are done by men. Decision-making at every step is also dominated by men.

The gender based division of work in agriculture is a logical outcome of the dominant social beliefs and attitude that define current status of women.

7.1.2 Major Barriers Faced by Women

Our survey revealed that women in the study areas face several barriers in their effective participation and in realizing their potential. The important ones are structural and thus are quite formidable like lack of ownership and effective control of land and other means of production, residential spaces, other assets and restricted mobility. Despite the laws facilitating women's ownership of land, women's actual land ownership is almost negligible and is primarily a force of circumstances like widowhood and an absence of men in the family. Joint ownership of land is not typically practised.

The study finds a strong and direct relationship between the structural barriers women face and dominant beliefs and attitudes that impact women at an individual as well as at social level. These feed into each other. The women's role within the farming system is entrenched in the patriarchal system. Women's roles are by and large guided by the social norms that give them a secondary position after men. The larger social value system dominates the overall psyche of women and men. Traditional values are the biggest barriers in equal participation of women, especially in the areas outside the home like marketing and skill-building which are dependent on education and training, controlling resources and undertaking managerial functions.

These structural barriers lead to other problems like a double work burden, gender-based division of work, drudgery of work, non-participation in decision-making, domestic violence, lack of education and so on.

Control over women is perpetuated through wide-spread domestic violence, male ownership and control over assets and outputs, and men's higher levels of education. The control of men over women in the study areas is *de jure* as well as *de facto*.

Women-Headed Households are Not Better Off

The number of women-headed households is increasing. During the course of study, we came across several instances where a man in the household is economically inactive yet heads the family and resorts to domestic violence to exert control. Merely earning income does not make a woman head of the household. A man is the head of the household in Indian society by default. A woman becomes head only in cases when men are not around. Thus, women-headed households are not a matter of choice but of extenuating circumstances like widowhood, male-migration, desertion, et cetera. Consequently, women heads of households face the general barriers other women face.

7.1.3 Women Suffer from Double Work Burden

The status of women is changing. This has been recognized by women as well as by others. This change is evident in many aspects of society—access to education, interactions with others outside work, ownership of land and general mobility. However, the pace of change is not only slow but too small to make a perceptible change in gender power dynamics.

Not all changes, however, benefit women. For instance, the change in women's status from domestic worker to farmer-cum-domestic worker has certainly increased women's work burden. Women's increasing participation in agricultural activities, whether out of choice or compulsion, is not without cost. Several women reported this additional burden of work with increased agricultural work.

Women farmers are thus doubly burdened with domestic as well as agriculture work. A woman farmer on an average works for almost 15 to18 hours a day. Men in contrast work on an average for 6 to 8 hours. This is also true for girls for whom education has not brought any respite from domestic chores.

7.1.4 Role of the State

Our findings related to extension services suggest that none of the farm women surveyed benefited from the existing government extension services. The reach of extension services to marginal and small farmers appear to be negligible. Presently the extension services also tend to be not only male-biased but also scale-biased.

Men and women both find other welfare programmes quite useful. At the same time, they find it difficult to extract benefits from the programmes because of the high level of corruption in the system. Such corruption has been noted not only for schemes where there is restricted access, but also for legal universal entitlement schemes like MNREGA. A deeper analysis, however, suggests that there are several structural reasons that render various programmes ineffective. The important ones include restricted access, lack of accountability and monitoring, gender biases, et cetera.

The government welfare programmes are, in a nutshell, ill-conceived, discriminatory and poorly implemented. Consequently, they have no significant impact on women's status. Awareness about the provisions of gender-friendly laws, policies and programmes is low and implementation extremely weak. In totality, it appears that the state is deliberately ineffective as far as the pro-poor programms are concerned. There is no public pressure from below for effective implementation.

7.1.5 The Sources of Women's Power: Participation in Decision-Making, Control over Products and Incomes

Additional agricultural work has not added to women's status or self-esteem in most cases. This is because they have no control over the fruits of their labour. Our study suggests that women have greater control over kitchen gardens, which are totally controlled by women. A kitchen garden is therefore a source of pride among the women. It is their own. They have control over the produce as well as the proceeds from sales. Though only some of the survey participants referred to having kitchen gardens, the research suggests that they offer women a means to make decisions and exert control over products and income—an important feature for women's self-esteem.

The other independent source of income for women in the study area over which they have full control is MNREGA. This is, however, regionally-specific.

Legal frame and contestation is another source of power. Through contestations, women can acquire ownership of means of production and improve their situation. Another important source of power is in the membership of a group like a SHG or a cooperative. However we do not have reported instances of this group membership in the research areas.

7.1.6 Contestation and Charting Newer Paths: Role Models Show the Path Forward

Seeds of change are visible. Several women resolutely said that they are capable of doing men's work but because of social barriers and being over burdened they refrain from doing so.

Despite all barriers, several women have taken up the challenge and have worked hard to chart a different path for themselves. Though hard work may have taken a toll on them, they carry forward their struggle for a better life, especially for the children including girls. These examples are indicators of changing possibilities. Awareness, education and training seem to be important motivators for women to chart out a different path.

Several women from male-headed households—have reported to be doing the entirety of farm activities by themselves, including market-related work and yielding good outcomes. The work is as a manager farmer in the real sense of the term.

Box 7.1: Role Model: Laxmi Devi

She is from the family of Shri Ramlakhan. She does timely agriculture work. She keeps information about new seeds and techniques. She got trained about two years ago by the horticulture department. She got a poly tunnel for setting up a tomato-seed nursery. She used this technique for production of tomatoes and reaped a very good crop. She sold tomatoes worth 24 thousand rupees.

Source: Focus group discussions, men, Hussainpur, Shahjahanpur

7.2 Constraints and Opportunities

7.2.1 Constraints

(i) Lack of Ownership of Resources

Agriculture work requires several material resources in addition to labour. The important material resources include land, water, equipment and machinery, inputs like seed, fertilizer, pesticide, credit. The ownership of these resources determines the use. It is the owner who decides which crop to sow, which seeds and fertilizers to be used, how much and where to sold the produce, how to use the money and so on. To illustrate, if the land is cultivated by someone who does not own it, there would be no investment in land affecting its productivity adversely. Similarly, women cannot be expected to invest heavily in a piece of land that is not owned by them. To quote from a study:

> Inequality in the distribution of resources between men and women is linked to production inefficiency, yet interventions targeting small holder farmers often fail to redress women's lack of access to, and control of, important agricultural resources. Women are often constrained in access to and control of land, water, and other natural resources; complementary inputs, such as seeds and fertilizers; new varieties and technologies; agricultural extension; labour; credit; markets; and social capital.

The findings of the study suggest that women have no ownership of means of production. The ownership and control of resources reside with the male in the family.

(ii) Lack of Mobility

Lack of mobility is yet another important crucial social constraint that adversely affects the status of women. The question of mobility is directly related to women's future status as well. The study indicates that restrictions on mobility today puts limits on opportunities for girls tomorrow. Though girls are provided formal education, the opportunities provided are limited compared to boys, including that girls are often not sent for education if it is beyond the village boundaries.

The restricted mobility is equally crucial for the present generation of women as well. The lack of mobility adds and perpetuates their secondary position as they lack access to and control over incomes.

(iii) Gender based Division of Work

The third important constraint is the gender division in work. The division is primarily based on status. There is a dialectic relationship between the status and work division. Traditional roles on the basis of gender are rooted in the status of women and continuation of their existing roles, which in turn, perpetuate the secondary status of women. Thus, this constraint has to be dealt with simultaneously with others.

(iv) Double Work Burden

One important constraint meaningful participation of women in agriculture work is the double work burden. Women's domestic work load does not get reduced when agricultural work gets added to their portfolio. Thus agricultural work increases their working time.

(v) Lack of Collectives

Another important constraint relates to the exposure of women to collectives or affiliation with women's groups. To affect change in women's status, they would have to wield power, the source of which lies in collectives of one or the other type. The question of status relate to 'the women' and not 'a woman'. The status of women in the home is only a 'micro' reflection of a 'macro' social reality. Status of women is a social problem and accordingly the solution too has to be social.

(vi) Lack of Empowering Approaches in the Government Programmes

The role of the state is important in any social effort of change. There are innumerable programmes of the government in the agriculture sector. Unfortunately, most of the programmes have faulty designs in that they do not lead to women's empowerment. Women are given compulsory access to programmes which do not necessarily empower women as most are either gender- neutral or framed with dominant gender ideology.

7.2.2 Opportunities

There are opportunities available at various levels and in different forms for raising the status of women. Women can draw benefits from those opportunities by individual as well as collaborative efforts.

(i) The Broad Favorable Environment

Today, there is a broad social environment which is gender-friendly and sex-based discrimination is becoming increasingly intolerable. Discriminatory practices are often more pronounced within the four walls of the households and within the confines of the communities. Outside of homes and communities, gender discrimination is vehemently looked down upon and despised. The media, the State, the politicians, the judiciary and the bureaucracy by and large stand for gender equality. Therefore the social environment is quite conducive for changes in the status of women.

(ii) Legal Opportunities

The biggest opportunities for women lie in the emerging women-friendly legal environment. There are several legal instruments available which need to be used to improve the status of women. At the top is the fundamental right guaranteed by the Constitution of India—the right to equality. These instruments need to be used to counter social practices. The important legal instruments include laws related to sex selection, property rights, domestic violence, right to education, employment guarantee, reservations at various levels, et cetera.

(iii) Programmatic Opportunities

In addition to legal opportunities, equally important if not more so are the opportunities offered by the plethora of state programmes aimed at ameliorating the conditions and status of women in general and women farmers in particular. Such programmes are available in both the central and state sphere. The important programmes in the central sphere are NRLM, NRHM, ICDS, PDS, et cetera. Within National Rural Livelihood Mission there is an entire component meant for empowerment of women farmers, in the name of MKSP, Mahila Kisan Sashaktikaran Pariyojana, there are several State sphere programmes as well.

(iv) Opportunities Offered by Role Models

In the project, we came across several women who have led the way towards improving the status of women by entering into male-dominated activities like buying seeds, fertilizers, using modern methods of crop raising, selling crops, managing money, acquiring ownership of land, educating daughters and so on. These role models are within the areas that form the basis for initiating, promoting and consolidating the change process.

(v) Women Initiatives

There are several organizations that are fighting for the rights of women for a more gender-friendly society. The mindset of the general society is changing, albeit at a slow pace. Local initiative is a required first step. Women need to take a step ahead and grab their rights.

7.3 Recommended Interventions

For any intervention to be effective it must be based on well-thought out strategies. Broadly speaking, two types of interventions are possible to empower women farmers, based on the findings of our study. Firstly, there are interventions that aim to change key structural drivers that create, promote and perpetuate gender inequalities among farm women. Secondly, there are interventions that relate, not to agency, but are part of well-being and are directed towards securing benefits from the state. Both these interventions are interrelated and feed into each other.

Extra attention needs to be paid to the gender outcomes of the interventions. In fact, we propose an intervention framework that in its very structure takes into consideration gender outcomes and structural inequity. In the absence of such a framework it is likely that the intervention may reinforce gender discrimination rather than addressing it. In that case, even if households prosper, gender discrimination would continue and women would not enjoy the equality of opportunities in education and employment.

In more concrete terms, we find that specific interventions are required so that women gain equality of opportunity in education and work. This means that women share equally the ownership of assets including means of production, participate equally in decision-making at all levels and men share domestic work equally. The relationship between men and women would change from one based in dependence and domination to one grounded in interdependence and liberty. This has to be an overall goal of interventions. This is possible only when an integrated approach to development is taken. A piecemeal approach may not work as most of the issues are closely interwoven.

As we stated at the beginning of this chapter, the primary actor in such a change strategy has to be the women themselves and others should play a facilitating role only. It is from this perspective that we shall outline some of the interventions.

7.3.1 Creation of a Resource Centre

The most important need women farmers have, according to the research findings, is to have immediate access to key resources. Women farmers would benefit from a resource facility that is close in proximity and provides farming resources as well as personal guidance and help. This help could be in relation to the crop to be grown, seed to be used, type and quantity of fertilizers and pesticides to be applied, sowing time and technique to be used and so on. It could be in relation to problems related to access to government programmes like the employment programme, ration, pension, credit card, insurance and so on. And it could be in relation to inter-personal relations, education of girls, domestic violence, the role of community, the problem of dowry, et cetera. Thus, we conceive this centre as a platform for women and men to learn, to reflect, to plan action and to execute their plans individually and collectively.

Such a facility/resource needs to be created in collaboration with the community with a clear understanding that it would be managed by the community in a self-sustaining manner. Men have to be taken into account, but the facility should be managed by women. The other values and operative principles for outsiders should be that no tangible benefit would be provided to the concerned community that create directly or obliquely any kind of dependence. Such a platform could be informal to begin with and may be initiated by some outside institution as part of the program.

7.3.2 Establishing Women's/Farmers' Collectives/Cooperatives

Establishing women farmer collectives would be a step forward. The women farmers are located at the bottom in the hierarchy of general interests. Their bargaining position is weak within and outside the home. This could also be said about small and marginal farmers. An effective way to give them a voice would be to set up collectives. Such collectives could be promoted on the basis of commonality of interests. To begin with, one agenda could be mutual labour sharing. Another could be bargaining with local self-government for ration cards for all the women-farmers. Yet another could be sustainable production and/or marketing of products. However, what is important is the exploration of the idea with the women farmers and then helping them proceed with their own agenda.

The beginning could be, depending upon the perceived needs and the facilitating factors, a call by a concerned group of women for getting their daughters higher education or fighting the menace of the dowry, or admitting the girls in the same school as boys, or fighting dress codes and allowing girls to wear jeans. The role of outsiders should be restricted to facilitation. The resource centre referred to above may be a platform to promote such collective(s). It could be developed on the lines of need-based cooperatives like producers or marketing cooperatives. Such cooperatives, however, should be based on a set of values and operating principles such that solidarity emerges rather than competition.

At the initial stages, these collectives will have to focus on promoting among the women farmers an 'outside-the-box' thinking process. Women should be able to critically think about the social processes and cultural practices that have kept them subjugated for long. They need to understand that these iniquitous arrangements are not 'supernatural' and can be changed. This is a prerequisite for unleashing a process of empowerment as defined in the Annexure A. For this purpose an appropriate communication strategy should be developed based on credible sources of information, that may incorporate differences prevailing in different groups.

7.3.3 Revamping of Extension Services

The findings show the inadequacies and gender and scale biases in the current State-sponsored system of agricultural extension services. Though of late there has been some attention to women especially in training, the system largely remains gender biased. The training reach is low, number of women extension workers is non-existent, training is geared towards reinforcing traditional activities that women perform, the focus seems to be more on new value additions rather than empowering women within the existing production process and so on.

The extension services have to become gender-sensitive participatory practices. The reach has to be universal for small and marginal farmers. The important suggestions for extension services are:

(i) Male Extension Workers Should Be Trained to Meet the Specific Needs of Female Farmers

The gender division of labour by crop and task, although not static, means that female and male farmers often have different extension needs. Currently, most extension services focus on crops and activities controlled and performed by male farmers. Accordingly, it is important to make sure that the extension workers are trained in extension methods and communication skills suitable for female farmers and in tasks usually done by women.

(ii) Extension Services at the Doorstep

Keeping in view the fact that women have dual responsibility within and outside home, more training should be organized at the village level for their convenience. Extension agents also need to be equipped with adequate transportation so that they can travel to female farmers, because women are often unable to attend training outside their villages due to several social limitations

(iii) Recruit and Train Female Extension Workers

In the present research area, wherein the seclusion process is deep rooted, it is necessary to have a separate cadre of women who can work with the women farmers. This cadre of women extension workers needs to be sensitized on social nature of all gender based discrimination so that they are empowered in themselves and give empowering messages in all their interactions with women.

(iv) Provide Extension Messages in the Simplest Way Possible

A thoughtful communication strategy is very important for effective communication. Given the fact that most of the workers are either illiterate or have minimal education, the extension messages must be delivered in the simplest terms possible. The training materials should be easily understood. The training material should also be carefully developed so that it dosen't missor the dominant gender ideology, rather establishes women's identity as independent and confident farmers.

(v) Use Informal Networks for Information Diffusion

Information diffusion takes place only in part through formal extension services. Social networks play an important role, especially for women, who often have less access to formal channels of dissemination. Yet, as male and female networks often differ, extension information should be disseminated through the different networks.

(vi) Increase the Number and Coverage

To ensure that farm women get a fair deal from extension workers, there should be a sizeable number of well-trained women personnel in the extension programmes of agricultural development agencies at all levels, and especially at the grass-root level.

(vii) Special Courses and Schemes

As a long term measure, we would like to make the following three specific suggestions: (a) specific courses on gender and agriculture/forestry/fishery should be designed for inclusion in graduate programmes. This should be included as a stream of specialization at the postgraduate level; (b) there should be special schemes to include women agriculture graduates as extension workers. These women extension workers should further promote development of women workers in agriculture; (c) provisions should be made for promoting girls to study agriculture at school and college level.

7.3.4 Securing Benefits from State-sponsored Programmes: Recommended State Interventions

Another set of interventions relate to appropriate policy regime and effective delivery of various government programs/schemes both in the area of agriculture and other welfare areas such as quality education for children particularly girl child, PDS, MNREGA, Social Security et cetera.

(i) Suggestions for General Policy Regime and Other Government Interventions

As we found during our study, the current development policy has failed. There is a need for a clear policy so that there are no structural problems in the way of effective interventions.

The explicit goal of agricultural policy and programmes should be to improve the conditions of the farmer households in question rather than improve farm productivity alone. Securing livelihood is more important in the face of the current agrarian crisis. To address the crisis, it is important to adopt alternate forms of agricultural practices and reform institutions. Both are interlinked. The issue of agriculture needs to be looked at more from the livelihood of those involved rather than from commercialization and marketable surplus.[23] This paradigm shift in institutions and agricultural practices certainly would not compromise feeding the non-agriculture population.

The primary goal of such a policy shift should be to ensure food security/secure livelihoods through the promotion of sustainable agriculture for the rural mass of small and marginal farmers and other agricultural workers. And the focal point of reorganization of agriculture should include local production, local procurement, local storage and local distribution mechanism alongside gender equity.

Secondly, the agricultural policy should have gender equality as an explicit goal. This is important even from the point of view of overall development. A recent study by International Labour Organization, for instance, observed that economic security is worsened by policies and institutions which do not realize that promoting women's control over their incomes and resources would help boost growth and development. This is one of the 'main forms of gender inequality across the world' (ILO, 2004: p. 86) and is systematically neglected in social policy and income statistics.

It is essential, therefore, that programmes and policies are so designed that, women are (a) bestowed with effective control and ownership of land, (b) made technologically empowered, (c) skilled in enhancing of agricultural management, and (d) imparted with knowledge of agriculture.

This should increase agricultural production and reduce poverty and income inequality. Each and every policy/ programme should be vetted accordingly.

In this context, we would like to emphasize that the value addition-related interventions should aim to place the control of product and output/sale proceeds with the women/ producers. The value additions should be based on women's traditional knowledge. The control over supply should rest with farmers/women and not on agribusiness or other outsiders. For this, it is necessary that the state or non-profit social organizations provide for and/or facilitate necessary platforms and help.

With regard to other programmes, firstly, policy should move towards universal coverage. The study shows that the targeted programmes feed into traditional systems and exclude the needy. It is necessary that the programmes related to food and social security are made universal. Secondly, appropriate systems of accountability need to be put in place alongside deterrent punishment. Thirdly, the processes should be made simple and transparent.

(ii) Some Specific Government Interventions

Our survey recommends the following:

- *(a) A Special Mission for Promoting Land ownership in the Name of Women:* There is a need for actualizing the legal ownership of land in the name of the women as soon as possible. To facilitate the process a special mission needs to be set up. An extensive programme for legal awareness and legal support to women should be part of this mission.
- *(b) Access to Institutional Credit:* Our study suggests that women do more farm work but Kisan Cards are in men's name. We strongly recommend that all the Kisan Cards should be jointly named and in the sole name of women who de facto manage agriculture because of migration or death or desertion. Moreover, the Kisan Cards should be given even to those farmers who do farming with leased-in land. In order to meet the credit needs of the

small and marginal farmers, credit for the group should be earmarked.

(c) *Focused Extension and Marketing Initiatives:* We have discussed in detail the revamped extension services. Here, we only highlight the need for a mission approach for comprehensive extension services including education and skill development for women and small and marginal farmers and strategies for need-based sustainable access to extension services like *Asha* and *Aanganwadi Worker* for health and nutrition.

(d) *Promotion of Awareness and Group Initiatives:* Awareness and group initiatives need to be promoted. As suggested in the agricultural policy of 2007, small farmer estates and/or cooperatives should be promoted through incentives and special programmes.

(e) *Compulsory Crop Insurance:* The reach of crop insurance is negligible. It should be made mandatory and universal.

(f) *Simplified and Transparent Procedure*: Procedural formalities regarding benefit of schemes should be simplified and made user-friendly, keeping in mind the illiteracy level. They should be transparent and time bound. Records should be accessible online as to who applied when and for what, and what happened, so that anyone can verify at any time.

(g) *Universal Social Security:* All the small and marginal farmers should be covered under universal social security providing health expenses, life and unemployment insurance, maternity benefits and old age pension. Our study finds that a large number of farmers do not have an adequate means of livelihood. Any emergency drives the farmer household into a very difficult financial situation due to the lack of social security.

(h) *Universal PDS is Required:* Universal PDS would provide food security to the households. During our survey, the need for food security through a ration system was prominently articulated by several survey participants. In fact, the role of PDS in promoting agriculture is now increasingly emphasized.[24] The case of Chhattisgarh reveals that the universal PDS was helpful in achieving a high growth rate of five per cent compared to three per cent for India generally.

(i) State Interventions are Inevitable

It has often been argued that when there is poor implementation of the programmes, why should they be expanded? This is an important point that needs careful consideration. One important reason relates to targeting. For instance, in a country like India where per capita spending by 78 per cent of the population is Rs 20 or less per day, only 36 per cent have been identified for PDS and other benefits. The selection process is bound to be faulty. The only remedy for this could be universalization of the programme. Moreover, given the size and scale of the interventions required and the responsibility of the State towards its people, the programs cannot be put solely in the private domain.

(ii) Suggestions for Making Mandis Gender-friendly

These are some of the specific suggestions that were made during the course of study by different stake holders. At the outset, we suggest that women should be compulsorily included on the board of 'Mandi Samitis'.

The following suggestions, if implemented properly, could make the *mandis* gender-friendly: (a) women and men should get equal wages, (b) there should be a woman helper in the *mandi* who can help women in weighing and in negotiating rates, (c) there should be separate toilet facilities for women in the *mandis*, (d) there should be a storage area where produce can be kept if it is not sold completely that day.

7.3.5 Intervention Framework

We conclude this section by delineating a possible intervention framework. This only outlines certain possible interventions in terms of a scheme. It suggests that an intervention should be issue-specific and each intervention should have a precise goal, the source of realization of the goal, a strategy broadly in terms of level of action, and the likely impact in terms of agency or well-being. The listing in Table 7.1 is not comprehensive. Drawing a comprehensive list was not within the available means, though it is a distinct possibility. Women are in the centre of these interventions. Outsiders' role should be as facilitators only. The primary actors are women themselves. Thus these are situated in the empowerment frame.

Secondly, these individual interventions have to be part of an overall goal as discussed at the beginning of this section.

Table 7.1: Potential Intervention Framework: Indicative

Women Farmers Issue	*Goal*	*Source*	*Strategy*	*Likely Impact*
Cheap ration	BPL card for all farm-women	Central govt	Collective advocacy	Well-being-reduces food uncertainty
Farm-credit	Kisan card	Bank	Awareness and demand creation	Agency-control over money
Lack of employment during off season	Job card; non-farm employment	Pradhan	Demand job through application	Well-being-extra income
Lack of skills	Acquiring skills	Extension department	Demand training	Agency-skilling empowers
Lack of mobility	Going to market	Within: self-confidence and self -assertion	Resolution/ enlisting support of significant other members	Empowering-contesting and breaking social rules
Domestic violence	Elimination/ stopping violent behaviour	Husband/ elders/other males	Contestation/ protest: individual/ collective recourse to legal measures in extreme cases	Agency: equality/ respect
Lack of toilets	Creating toilet facilities at	Sanitation programme of govt/family	Demand/ perseverance	Well-being: important facility
Work burden	Gas facility for cooking	state/ family	Demand free gas cylinders for women farmers Advocacy through collectives	Well-being: labour-saving technology

8

Breaking the Grass Ceiling

Women Farmers strive for Equity and Dignity

The present monograph, as stated in the beginning, presents the findings of a baseline survey done to understand the current situation of the women farmers in select district of Uttar Pradesh with an objective of designing and implementing an action intervention programme to ameliorate the conditions of women farmers through education, skill development and empowerment. It was expected that the recommended set of interventions would lead to awareness and education, skilling, empowerment and better livelihood outcomes for the women farmers covered. This chapter briefly deliniates the intervention frame, processes and outcomes of the interventions during the two and half year period from 2010 to 2013.

8.1 The Intervention Framework

The intervention frame used was in line with what is recommended in Chapter. Baseline survey had suggested that women farmers lives in the study area are shaped by customs that are centuries old and are restrictive to women having an identity of their own. To rephrase the findings, the women predominantly lead a life wherein they are physically battered, mentally tormented and socially excluded, which prevents them from contributing or participating in society on equal terms with men. Deprived of education, health, nutrition and other opportunities to grow and prosper in general, women usually have low self-respect, self-confidence, and self-esteem.

The discrimination and suppression sets limits to their aspirations to an extent that they don't assert their existence as an individual. Compromised with the situation, majority find solace in whatever they have and get.

Based on the baseline survey report, a two-fold action intervention strategy was chalked-out and implemented. On the one hand, the women were provided agricultural skills and knowledge, and simultaneously on the other hand, processes to empower them were initiated. The goal of the empowerment strategy was to enhance the self-esteem and enable them to question the established value system and cultural arrangements. The focus was on collective exploration, reflection and actions. The role of outsiders was considered important but only as facilitators and the means used were education, knowledge, exposure and formation of collectives. The specific action interventions are provided in the next section.

8.2 The Interventions, Processes and Outcomes

8.2.1 The Process of Collectivization

The process of collectives started with formation of women farmers' interest groups of 25 to 30 members each. These concentrated on education and training of farm related functions. Each group identified a lead farmer.

The very first step—when a woman becomes the member of a group by virtue of her being a farmer—is itself an act that challenges the socially imposed and accepted principal decision maker and actor, a male. The next steps involving breaking traditional barriers to travel to different places to receive training and share their learnings back in the group were the decisive steps to move upward within the value chain and as well as in gaining a new social status in the community which is more equitable, dignified and significant. Later the newer forms of groups, Women Self-Help Groups[25] (SHG) emerged with added function of money transactions.

Till date, in the project area about 220 such groups have been formed each having a membership of ten to thirteen women. Thus, roughly about 2500 women have joined the groups. Women contribute small amounts of money every month, then use this money for credit purposes. Many of the SHGs have opened up a bank account and have taken loans from bank for productive as well as reproductive purposes.

To consolidate the powers of individual small groups into a collective power, the SHG Women have organized themselves in 14 clusters each consisting of 10 to 15 SHGs in the adjoining areas and then into a federation. The federation is managed by a board which includes one representative from each cluster. The federation is registered in the name of 'Vama Shakti' (meaning *Women's Strength*). For smooth regular functioning, every SHG cluster and the federation holds a monthly meeting. During these meetings, they share the issues around them and decide a course of action.

The collective consciousness of women helped them a lot in overcoming the barriers of social and cultural practices that lead to all the major predicaments in their lives.

8.2.2 Interventions related to Agriculture Knowledge and Skills

(i) Training on Agriculture Skills

For effective technical education in the area of agriculture the farmer groups elected their leaders (called lead farmers). This group of leaders was provided training as future trainers. It was expected that they in turn would act as change agents and provide training and support to other women in their groups, under supervision and regular follow up from extension agents appointed for the purpose.

The network of lead farmers was provided direct training on appropriate agriculture technologies including soil sampling and testing, field preparation, seed selection, raising nursery in controlled environment, interculture operations, integrated pest management, harvest and post harvest handling and marketing of produce. These lead farmers then provided training and support to other women in their group.

The technical training has helped several women farmer participants to use the newly acquired skills successfully enhancing both the agency and well-being aspect. For instance, Sadhna Tripathi of village Vishnupur has learnt all the technologies very sincerely. Earlier, she used to cultivate her small land of 0.1 acre, but last season, her family, motivated and energized by the new awareness and knowledge, took two acres of land on lease, just to cultivate vegetables. 'It gives me great satisfaction to see the beautiful fields and I enjoy working in field. My income has grown many times', says Sadhna. Similarly, educated up to class eight, Kamlesh of village Mirzapur has learnt testing the content of NPK (Nitrogen, Phosphate and Potash) in the soil sample and now offers services to people on a payment basis. She has now become an agriculture extension worker having her own independent income along with the knowledge.

(ii) Demonstration Plots

For field-based live training and education, demonstration plots—one for every 250 farmers—were also laid to exhibit new technologies such as raising nursey in controlled environment (eg shade net houses, plug tray nursery, low poly tunnel), drip irrigation, soil solarisation, staking, integrated pest management et cetera. The demonstration plots help women see the on field results of any technology. When the trained women explain to the community about the technologies being demonstrated in their plots, it gave a boost to their self-confidence and status in the society. Anarkali of village Thatheripur, for instance, hardly ever talked to anyone in the village. Ever since a shade net was installed on her field to demonstrate nursery raising in raised bed and in plug tray under controlled conditions, many people have started coming to her field and she confidently and proudly shares her knowledge with all those who visit her field. 'Even my relatives in other villages give me a call to learn about the newer things', says Anarkali.

(iii) Exposure Visits

To enhance the self-esteem and build confidence, another intervention in the form of exposure trips was planned and implemented. Such exposure visits were to the national and regional universities, government institutions, farmers' fairs and to the places where women have broken the social and cultural barrier to move forward. Women also received specialized trainings organized by Gobind Ballabh Pant University of Agriculture and Technology (GBPUAT), Department of Agriculture, Indian Institute of Vegetable Research (IIVR) and Central Institute of Medicinal and Aromatic Plants (CIMAP).

The exposure visits were quite a learning experience for the women. If some learning were motivating and thrilling, some others at the same time were disappointing. Some of the field notes of a facilitator who accompanied during these visits are worth quoting here:

> It was for the first time that a group of 35 women came from remote villages to a farmers' fair in GBPUAT, Pantnagar. It was probably the first time for university too to host a group of women farmers. The control room in the fair was announcing time and again—Kisan Bhaiyo (Farmer Brothers)! Women went to the control room to register their concern—though the things did not change in the next fair too.
>
> Women interacted with a lot of input suppliers including those of seeds, pesticides and farm machinery. They were thrilled to see a battery operated spray pump, a poratable hoe & rotavator for ploughing, systems of drip irrigation et cetera...Several of them bought seeds of various vegetables for cultivation back home. There was a camp for free dental checkup in the fair. All the women took the advantage of the opportunity. They also visited the Livestock Research Centre, Mushroom Cultivation Centre, Vegetable Research Centre, Crop Research Centre and Agro forestry Research centre.
>
> They stayed in common room of one of the girls hostel of the university and shared their utility spaces. I could arrange for an interactive meeting between the college girls and our women on 9th evening. A few girls, mostly doing Post Graduation, gathered to talk to 28 women. They talked a lot about each other's lives and perceptions.
>
> Women got the opportunity to learn how girls come out from far off places just to study and how they carry themselves confidently with the boys there. They were amazed to see so many girls riding bicycles and operating computers. Girls also got a chance to understand the lives and predicaments of rural women.

> After a conversation of about two hours they sang and danced together for more than an hour.

The experiences led to aspirations and thus the process of change got rooted in the psyche of the women. This happened irrespective of the age of the women. Responses of the women who went for the exposure visit aptly sum up the outcome of the experiences:

> 'I have seen the heaven on earth as I got the opportunity to eat in a roadside restaurant, which otherwise I had heard of only through men' said Manki Devi, 75.
>
> Imarti Devi said, 'I would like to send my granddaughter to a place like this for studying.'

8.2.3 Women Empowerment Trainings

The first step in empowering women is the development of a critical consciousness in order to recognize: that the culture of silence is created to oppress; that the gender and other social relations are not given; and that the things can be challenged and changed. To be empowered in a real sense, it is very important that they gain freedom, not only to act but also to question and to reassess.

To take optimum advantage of the available opportunities to full potential, it is necessary that the predicaments that keep the women oppressed at several levels are addressed. Also important is that women themselves stand up to fight for the removal of inequities entrenched in the social systems. Thus, training on gender, rights and collective action were done at several levels to help women critically understand the systems and institutions that keep them deprived and to raise their consciousness for asserting their rights. Specifically, these trainings helped them realise that they are independent human beings with sovereign identity. They also recognized that all their sufferings are subject to social causes and can be challenged. Collective action became the way to change the *status quo*.

These trainings varied from one day to three day to six day depending upon the need of the group. For those who could not participate in residential trainings, a series of one day gender trainings was organized. In each one of them 30-35 women would get together at one place and the facilitator would have interactive exercises and discussions with them. The focus was on three specific messages—a) women matter b) their work is important and c) they have right over the family income. Women enjoyed these trainings a lot. 'For the first time there is someone who hear us women', says Meena, in one such traininig.

The cluster leaders were also provided training on issues related to: women's health; contesting violence; systems of governance through Panchayati Raj; and their entitlements in social security schemes. One important training that cluster leaders participated in was on 'Non-Violent Communication.' This helped women empathize with each other and helped them work together harmoniously. These leaders then share their learning and knowledge with other women during the cluster meetings and the cluster members then share it with the SHG women. This mechanism helps disseminate any information and learning to the entire group of women. An understanding of their rights and entitlements coupled with the collective strength improved women's bargaining power and positioned them to better negotiate spaces for themselves. There are several cases to prove this. Some are given below.

The long veil to cover her head used to annoy Seeta of village Thatheripur. In the wake of gender training, when she realized that a veil is not something mandated by 'God' and that it only limits her reach, she decided to raise it. Her friends were with her and that gave her the courage to be with her decision. Initially, her family members, including her husband, objected but she did not succumb to any pressure. It has a cascading effect as gradually many women have started emulating her. Shedding off the veil increased Sita's mobility and she became a teacher in the learning centre. That helped her better learn and adopt the agriculture technologies and made her a role model in the community. 'Nothing can stop me now from moving ahead', says Sita.

Similarly, Sudevi, 27, of village Todarpatti was a widow

for nine months when she came for one such training. She was in s state of total despair. The customary practices attached to widowhood had made her believe that life had closed all its doors on her. During the training, she realized that she was not responsible for her widowhood and that even if her husband was not with her, she had a life to live. The realization opened new doors for her. She smiled, she laughed, she sang, she danced, she wore colored clothes...and that changed her life. Gradually, she became the teacher of a learning centre and also got elected a member of the board of Vamashakti. She also got the opportunity to participate in a 20-day long training on when she and one of her friend went to Himachal Pradesh for 20 days training on gender and sustainable development. Seeing a widow in such colours and confidence was new for the area, but it set the aspirations of many other widows in the areas. 'Rules are made by us, and it is us who will have to differentiate the right from the wrong of these rules and make our choices,' says Sudevi. She also took initiative, and with her friends from Vamashakti, called for a meeting of widows in the area. The discussions gave all the women an opportunity to relate to each other owing to their specific sufferings. She is still trying hard to bring colours to lives of other women.

Kanchan and a few women in her farmer group wanted to raise a tomato nursery in raised beds. Since their families were not ready to support them in their new initiative, they together took a small piece of land on lease and raised nursery and crop collectively. Once they proved that the technology they adopted shows results, all the families in the next season adopted the same. During the celebration of International Women's Day, Kanchan and her group staged a play on the issues of domestic violence by close family members. 'The group women thought it is an issue concerning all women and girls and we need to raise our voice. There could not be a better platform for us to raise this issue', explains Kanchan.

8.2.4 Saksham – the Functional Literacy Centers

Literacy, as a variable relating to women's agency plays an important role in promoting social well being. It tends to make them better informed and functionally more powerful. UN Secretary General Ban Ki Moon, in his message on International Literacy Day 2010, said that 'Literacy has the capacity to "unlock capacity of individuals". It is not just reading and writing – it is about respect, opportunity and development.'

Most of the literature for agriculture is usually found in technical language which is difficult for rural women to understand. Realising the gap, some women conceptualized and developed small booklets on agriculture technologies for the neo-literate women. These booklets are written in their own vernacular language, used bold letters and enough pictures to support the text. The pictures and the text both ascertain the identity of women as independent farmers. 'It's is unbelievable. That I can write books is something I had never thought off' says Sita, a contributor to the booklet.

After the gender training, women wanted to raise their abilities and showed interest in getting literate. A quick field survey substantiated the feasibility and 20 literacy centres in the name of '*saksham*' (meaning able) were established. The objective of the program was to create an environment where women demand knowledge and information, empowering themselves to change their lives. For literacy to indeed be empowering and transformative, the education process should connect with women's lived realities. It should help women confront the challenges they face in their daily lives. Nirantar, a New Delhi based resource agency for Gender and Education helped in setting up literacy courses and learning centres. Being actively involved with the women's movement and other democratic rights movements, Nirantar brings concerns central to these movements into its educational work.

The literacy classes have given women an opportunity to break the isolation which is socially structured into their lives, giving them a chance to meet other women and learn collectively-rather than learn singly as individuals. All through their life they have lived the curse of being illiterate and that had taken their self image so down that they would always say 'I am not literate, so I cannot tell you anything.' People in the community would time and again say 'these women are not literate, they will not be able to understand anything.' But women's participation in the learning centres—both as educators and as learners—broke these stereotypes and created a new picture of women.

It provided teachers as well as learners with the enormous opportunities to learn and to step ahead. Besides the writing and numeracy skills they have an enhanced self image, heightened social awareness, higher confidence, increased mobility and placed then at better negotiating positions. Some of the educators have restarted their educational journey. For example, those who have passed class eight have applied for examination of class ninth and henceforth. This has led to instances of women countering violence at home and at public places. To dare do this, women certainly need to have a lot of courage from within.

In addition to their participation in the farmer groups, the centres gave women a platform to talk about any problem related to agriculture too. The literacy and numeracy skills helped them read the name of the seed on seed packets, their Maximum Retail Price (MRP), their expiry date. They could also read small information that was given through leaflets. They could do small calculations to determine the seed/ fertilizer rate or a pesticide dose. Since they do go out and interact with people, they are better aware of the market prices. The awareness and the confidence position them in a better place to negotiate prices and earn or save better.

8.2.5 Women and Farmer Resource Centre

Yet another intervention, as per the suggested strategy (Section 7.3.1), relate to setting up of dual platforms : Women Resource Centre (WRC) and Farmer Resource Centre (FRC). Housed at the same place it is called 'Vamakul' (meaning a place for women). Vamakul was set-up to create a space where women can meet regularly, discuss and chalk out need-based strategies and action plans. The place has a small library of literature related to women concerns and problems they face on daily basis.

Vamashakti is managed by women SHGs and plays an important role not only in imparting education and training but also in providing specific help to the farmers in getting agriculture inputs and implements at a reasonable price and at the right time. It also provides machinery like sprinklers, sprayers, irrigation pipes etcetera on rent and fee based services like soil testing and crop advisory.

Recently, Vamashakti has started facilitating access to the government programs and schemes. For example, if an eligible woman wants benefit of 'Old Age Pension Scheme', she can walk into Vamashakti and request for the same. The Centre facilitates the entire process beginning from application to receipt of first installment on a token charge. Such need-based facilitation is a great help to the needy and deprived.

8.2.6 Linkages with Markets and Institutions

The increased strength of women to overturn the iniquitous social arrangements, paved way for many collective interventions and linkages. These linkages led to realization of increased income and an awareness of rights helped them have control over its utilization.

Farmers in this area are growers of aonla (*Indian gooseberry*). Most of the people have 2-4 trees of aonla in their backyard. This remained untapped high-potential for income generation. To avoid transportation costs and price volatility in wholesale markets, it was a standard practice for farmers to lease out their crops to middlemen for a small given sum. To tap the potential for higher income, a collection centre for aonla, managed by women, was established in the area for direct sale. This has doubled their incomes. Similarly, Vegetable Collection Centres have also been established. These collective efforts have given them increased money and also established their presence in markets. Some women have also created history in the area by selling vegetables on pushcarts.

These efforts on one hand are breaking the stereotypes of women and on the other, increasing the roles of women in markets that are otherwise a male bastion. The benefits relate to both agency and well-being aspects.

8.2.7 Opportunities through Organization of Events

The set of interventions related to creation of opportunities for women to understand, explore, discuss and express themselves. An effort was made to create platforms where they could look critically into their own lives and raise voice for their own concerns.

(i) 'International Women's Day Conference

In March 2012, Vamashakti- celebrated the International Women's Day through a conference on the theme, 'Voices of Change'. The conference was planned, managed and controlled by the women themselves. During the three-hour-long event, women staged plays, shared incidents of their struggle, the change they are seeing into their lives, sang songs and enjoyed being themselves. Around 1500 women who participated had travelled on their own from far off places to participate in the event. Women played leadership roles, took collective responsibility and created their own spaces to raise voice on their own concerns.

(ii) Participation in the OBR Campaign

'One Billion Rising' (ORB) is an international campaign to catalyse communities, collectives, groups and individuals across the spectrum to raise voices and say no to any forms of violence. Vamashakti ran a discussion and signature campaign in all the fourteen clusters and also networked with other Women Rights organizations to organized events on 14th February, 2013 the final day of the campaign. This rejuvenated all the people in the community and brought to forefront the various forms of violence that women face. Not only women, other members of community participated in the discussions and showed their concurrence to say no to all forms of violence against women.

(iii) Organization of Women farmers' Fair

Various agriculture universities and the government departments regularly organize farmer's fair to disseminate new technologies to farmers. However, participation of women farmers in such fairs is negligible. Even if they manage to physically participate, the mediums of exhibitions and communication are not as per the needs of women. Recognising this gap, Vamashakti organized an all-Women Farmers' Fair on 28 Feb 2013. A total of 45 stalls were laid by various NGOs, input supply companies, government departments and institutions. Vamashakti had laid stalls on agriculture technologies. These stalls were facilitated by women for the visiting women. There were also puppet show, games, quiz programs and other fun and food stalls, all organized by women. Around 2500 women and 500 men from six adjoining district participated in the fair. The fair gave women an identity as a farmer and also served a platform where they can easily learn about the new technologies, available services and the government programmes.

8.3 Resolute Women Overcome Challenges

Two and half years of efforts of women farmers in the select areas of Pratapgarh to break the grass ceiling has not been smooth and there is a long way to go. It was daunting and despite several steps forward a great deal of task remains. The future, too, is not likely to be smooth as well, if not impossible.

The first challenge encountered was to make the women think about themselves. The way they are socialized they think about everyone else but themselves. It is so obvious in the very first interaction given below:

> 30 women had gathered for their first training on vegetable production. 'Please introduce yourselves,and say what your favourite food is,' I said.
>
> 'My son likes *samosa*' (a type of stuffed pastry), said one, 'and I eat it too.'
>
> 'Lentils and flat bread... anything that fills your stomach is good,' said another.
>
> 'When you are hungry, then everything is good', said a third.

The next challenge was to make women themselves receptive to the idea of 'women as independent farmers' (unlike the traditional notion of considering them as members of integrated household). The community resistance to the idea of women-centric agriculture interventions, in a men's world was expectedly quite formidable. Questions were hurled before the outside facilitators, 'Why with women? They are not farmers! They don't have land! They just don't know anything!' To make the community realize that women are farmers too was a difficult challenge. At times, it took long to convince a simple thing that women work on farm and have farming skills, thus they are farmers.

Low self-esteem of women was yet another initial road block. Often they would say 'We just can't understand anything. We are illiterate.' In one of the earliest meetings, I remember a woman who could not even remember her name. She got married at the age of seven, came to her marital home at 12 and ever since she was called not by her name but as her husband Ramlal's wife. That was the social reality of women to begin the journey. But the education and training finally paid off and gradually things started changing.

When women took their first step out of the rigid social norms, there were many instances of backlash and resistance from men as well as women within the family. Shahnaz, a lead farmer from Lachchipur, was badly beaten by her husband after she reached back home from the first training. But she chose not to opt out of the programme. 'If not this, he will have another reason to beat me. This time, I have firmly decided not to stop.' Her grit was real base for change. Today, she is the member of governing board of Vamashakti and her husband has started supporting her. At times, he himself drops her for the meeting on his cycle. Shahnaj is also learning to ride a bicycle so that she becomes independent to move to different places.

One of the major learning of the program is that if women stand firm on their belief and do not take back their steps, gradually the same people, from the same community who opposed tend to respect them and create supportive environment. The experiences also suggest that women are more resolute. Vinay, Kanchan's husband, on the occasion of International Women' Day Celebration stood on stage before an audience of 1500, and said, ' Earlier, I did not support my wife but then through the gender trainings I learnt that women also are independent beings and it is important for them to move forward. Now I support her in all her efforts and encourage her not to feel dejected if someone in the village or the family says something bad.' Kanchan is a lead farmer and an educator in the learning centre. She contributed to writing of booklets for neoliterate women.

8.4 In Conclusion

The brief description of the experiences above clearly demonstrate that women have the courage, determination and the potential to change their status and well-being provided there is need-based facilitation to implement a programme based on education, skill building and empowerment.

The first and foremost thing required in case of women farmers is the self-esteem and self-confidence. The deprivation of women is linked primarily to the lower status of women which in turn lead to culture of silence and dependence. For a practical attempt at enhancing the well being of women, breaking this culture of silence has to be the first step and that is where the role of an outside agency becomes crucial.

The strategy should include, especially in the context of women farmers, processes of change for both empowerment and well-being. The outcomes of the interventions clearly establish the importance of both the aspects. Both feed into each other and help create a new status for women. The outcomes also underline the importance of mainstreaming of gender issues and proactive integration of gender components into broader agriculture development strategies. Equally important is the use of participatory empowering methods for gender awareness.

However, given the very nature of gender relations, there cannot be pre-determined specific line of action. Gender relations, like all other relations are multi stranded and inter-related power relations. They embody: ideas, values, and identities; they allocate labour between different tasks, activities and domains; they determine the distribution of resources; and they assign authority, agency and decision making power.

Consequently, a shift in one aspect of social relations can initiate a series of changes in other aspects leading to changed status and well being.

Thus, the distinct characteristics like women's earning power, economic role outside family, literacy and education, confidence and leadership etc may at first sight appear to be quite disparate and not linked with each other. But it is not so. They all are part of one outcome—the status of woman. The social status also determines the well-being not only of women but of the family and society in final analysis. The social and the economic empowerment go hand in hand in a cyclic manner. The ability to traverse the social constraints increases the ability to take advantage of economic opportunities and independent economic gains increase the bargaining power of women to negotiate social spaces for themselves. The story of interventions discussed above validates this.

For example, we noted above how life of a woman changed by her determination to raise her veil. This one act of courage gave her the confidence to face family and community, opened up the opportunity to do market related work and have independent income. This consequently improved her bargaining power to claim herself and led to increased participation in decisions of the household, including farming decisions.

The diverse variables that enhance women's social capability and effectiveness thus have empowering roles, both individually and jointly. The outcomes could improve their skills in agriculture, make them confident of themselves and their technical skills, improve their literacy skills, increase their reach to market spaces, encourage them to work collectively, and give them the conviction to challenge the social norms. Then only will women be able to recognize their own voice, decide on the priorities, have great control of their own lives and be able to realize their self-hood in full measure.

The project interventions helped empowerment of women at different levels: at the individual level, women's perceptions about their own self and their occupation has increased; at a group level, they have given strength to each other in challenging the iniquitous and entrenched practices that are often accepted as supernaturally ordained; and at a societal level, a too, they could generate a discourse and create tangible impressions on what is possible and impossible for women to do and how women should behave.

The women farmers in the area of intervention still face resistance of different nature and degrees from their family members, community and the institutions but they will certainly find out ways to deal with them. A group of women has emerged who should be able to sustain the change process even without the presence of outside facilitators. This is the primary outcome of the interventions.

NOTES

1. Abundant research material is available on agrarian crises, farmers distress and farmers suicides in India. See, for instance, Reddy and Mishra (2010), NCEUS (2007), NCW (2005).
2. As per Census 2011, of total main workers in rural India 70.68 per cent workers were reported as agricultural workers either as cultivators or as agricultural labourers. In the case of total marginal workers the corresponding percentage is even higher at 72.28. Calculated from Table A-5-Union Primary Census Abstract. See: Census (2013).
3. The green revolution of the seventies in India was based on betting on the strong. It only increased the regional and household level inequities as well added the problems related to sustainable development. Ample literature is available on this.
4. India's growth rate has been consistently high during last 15 years or so. The growth has not been inclusive though. The majority has not benefitted from this. The high inequalities forced the India government to make inclusive growth primary objective of the 11th and 12th plan.
5. While releasing a report on Hunger and Malnutrition, popularly known as HUNGaMA report on 10th January 2012, Dr Manmohan Singh, Prime Minister of India stated that "... the problem of malnutrition is a matter of national shame." (Indian Express, 2012a).

6. In a written answer to a question in the Rajya Sabha, the State Minister for Agriculture Mr Harish Rawat informed that as per official records a total number of 290470 lakhs of farmers have committed suicides during 1995 to 2011. (Indian Express, 2012b)
7. This estimate has been arrived at on the basis of NSSO data for the year 2004-05 by the National Commission on Enterprises in the Unorganized Sector (NCEUS, 2007)
8. The continuing agrarian crisis and un-remunerative agriculture forced the government set-up a commission in 2004 under Prof M.S. Swaminathan. The report was submitted in 2006. Based on the report a new National Policy for Farmers was released in 2007. It began with the following statement: This Policy is intended to help in rejuvenating the farm sector and bringing lasting improvement in the economic condition of the farmers. The first provision was stated as: Focus to be on the economic well-being of the farmers than just on production and productivity and this is to be the principal determinant of Farmers policy. (PIB 2007)
9. Though this system is not solely responsible for the secondary position, it makes dependence on men absolute. Subordination of women is equally observed in places like southern India where the system in unknown. The essence of subordination lies in the property relations.
10. There are several studies available to substantiate this point. See for eg. NCEUS 2007, Deshingkar 2003.
11. Seasonal circular migration has acquired a serious proportion in India. There are no precise numbers but rough estimates by scholars suggest that a number of such migrants could be over one hundred million. The NCEUS reported 30 million seasonal migrants.
12. It has been argued by Breman and others that circular migration is forced on rural people. They go to urban areas for employment, however, the moment they complete their employment they are forced to go back to the village. The conditions in urban areas are hostile, and the terms of employment are designed in a way that migrants have no option but to return.
13. One of the plausible reasons for drastic decline in absolute number of female owner cultivators and increase in female

agriculture wage labourers in the 2011 over 2001, as data in Table 2.2 suggests is land acquisition by state and private agencies.

14. In this report, the word State with capital S refers to all legal institutions that control social relations through means of rules, regulations, policies, programmes, schemes, et cetera. It thus includes all elected bodies, administrative units and their subsidiaries, enforcing authorities, and judicial bodies. The role of State in defining, constructing and regulating social relations including gender relations is very important.
15. Command area is the area around a dam where the benefits of dam, such as water for irrigation, reach.
16. The leasing in/out is caused by two issues, which are both related to the unfinished agenda of land reforms. There are certain families who own land but do not cultivate themselves. Secondly, there are families who own land in several parcels situated at different locations. Such families lease out one parcel and lease-in another which they can manage to cultivate. So there is a problem of redistribution viability as well as consolidation of land.
17. A *kachha* building is one made of soft natural materials like sand, mud, thatch or sticks and therefore is weak and short-lived structure.
18. The term *parda* has been used here in a wide sense to include all expressions that restrict mobility, freedom and women's choice.
19. Reported in a group interview in village Badavan, Shahjahanpur. The basis of the caste system in India relates to nature of work. The uneducated menial workers are lowest in the caste hierarchy.
20. In the recent past a major scam has been unearthed in the state of UP relating to diversion of ration cereals worth hundreds of millions of rupees. There is rampant corruption in the PDS system and even the Supreme Court of India is looking into the matter. The PDS system in India, and especially in states like UP, requires complete restructuring to make it people-friendly.
21. Section 19 of the Food Security Bill 2011 introduced in Indian-Parliament has this provision (GOI 2011).
22. MDM is a universal supplementary nutrition programme

under which cooked-meal is provided in school to every government and aided school student of Class 1 to 8 during the recess.

23. This view is contradictory to the dominant development philosophy view wherein the emphasis is solely on commercialization.
24. The role of PDS in sustainable agriculture has been effectively argued by the Right to Food Campaign. The Chhattisgarh experiment is a living testimony to this argument.
25. A Self-Help Group here refers to a group of 10-15 women in a village, who come together for addressing their common problems. They make voluntary thrift on a regular basis and use this pooled resource to make small interest bearing loans to their members.

References

Agarwal, Bina, 1998, *A Field of One's Own: Gender and Land Rights in South Asia*, Cambridge University Press, Delhi.

Agarwal, Bina, 2003, Gender and Land Rights Revisited: Exploring New Prospects via the State, Family and Market in Razavi, Shahra ed. (2003) *Agrarian Change, Gender and Land Rights*, UNRISD and Blackwell, UK, pp. 184-224.

Aggarwal Meenu, 2003, *Economic Participation of Rural Women in Agriculture* in Economic Empowerment of Rural Women in India, by Gopal Singh (ed.), RBSA Publications, Jaipur, Rajasthan.

Census, 2013, *Primary Census Abstracts 2011*, downloaded from the official web site of Census of India. Source: http://www.censusindia.gov.in/2011census/hlo/PCA_Highlights/pca_highlights.html

Chaudhary, Sarmishta, 2004, Invisible Activities of Rural Women, *Kurukshetra*, Vol. 52 , No. 9.

Cherian, A., A. Vats and C. Dixit, 2000, Work Profile of Rural women of Udham Singh Nagar of Uttar Pradesh, *Indian Farming*, November, pp. 31–34.

Deshingkar, Priya and Daniel Start, 2003, *Seasonal Migration for Livelihoods in India: Coping, Accumulation and Exclusion*, Working Paper 220, Overseas Development Institute, London

Economic Survey, 2010, Finance Ministry, Government of India.

Food and Agricultural Organization of the United Nations (FAO), 2006, *"A Perspective on Gender and Land Rights"*, Rome.

Government of India, 2001, *National Policy for Empowerment of Women, Department of Women and Child Development*. Source: http://wcd.nic.in/empwomen.htm

Government of India, 2006a, Serving Formers and Saving Farming in Third Report, *National Commission on Farmers*, Ministry of Agriculture, Delhi. PDF, pp. 1-311.

Government of India, 2006b, National Commission on Farmers, Ministry of Agriculture, Delhi. Source: http://agricoop.nic.in/ncf/ncf%20report%20-%203.pdf

Government of India, 2011, The National Food Security Bill 2011, Ministry of Food and Civil Supplies, New Delhi. Source:

Hardikar, Jaideep, 2004, *Migaration, Agriculture and Women*, India Together website.

ICAR, 2003, *DATABOOK on Women in Agriculture, AICRP(Home Science) Table on Decision making by women Independently for small farmers*, Indian Council of Agricultural Research, New Delhi.

Indian Express 2012a, *Problem of malnutrition a matter of national shame: Prime Minister, Jan 10*. Source: http://www.indianexpress.com/news/problem-of-malnutrition-a-matter-of-national-shame-prime-minister/898024/

Indian Express, 2012b, *2.90 lakh farmers committed suicide during 1995-2011 –Govt, August 31*, Source: http://www.indianexpress.com/news/2.90-lakh-farmers-committed-suicide-during-19952011-govt/995981/

International Land Coalition (ILC) and IFAD, 2004, *Voices from the Field*, India: Women's Resource Access Programme, Rome.

Kelkar, Govind, 2009, *The Feminization of Agriculture in Asia: Implications for Women's Agency and Productivity*, UNIFEM South-Asia Regional Office, New Delhi.

Kelkar, Govind, Dev Nathan and Pierre Walters (eds), 2003, *Gender Relations in Forest Societies: Patriarchy at Odds*, Sage Publications.

Kumar, Shiv and JPS Dhabas, 2002, *Impact of WTO on Seed Production* in H.S. Jat and Dhiraj Singh, Farmer's Forum Haryana State.

Kumar, Sunil, 2005, *Note on Farm Sector in Uttar Pradesh*, Department of Planning, Government of Uttar Pradesh, October.

Mencher, J.P., 1988, Women's Work, and Poverty: Contribution to Household Maintenance in Two Regions of South India in Dwyer, D. and J. Bruce (eds). *A Home Divided: Women and Income in the Third World*, Stanford University Press.

NCEUS, 2007. *Report on Conditions of Work and Promotion of Livelihoods in the Unorganized Sector*, New Delhi. (Mimeo)

NCW, 2005, *Impact of WTO on Women in Agriculture*, Research Foundation, Science and Technology, New Delhi. (Mimeo)

NCW, 2008, *Draft Agricultural Policy for Women*, Delhi

NSSO, 2004, 59th round, *Situation Assessment Survey of Farmers*, Government of India.

Oxfam, 2010, *India: Women Farmers Persevere*, Downloaded from Oxfam Website.

PIB, 2007, *National Policy for Farmers 2007*, Ministry of Agriculture,

Nov 27. Source: http://pib.nic.in/newsite/erelease.aspx?relid=33200

Reddy, D. Narasimha and Srijit Mishra, 2010, *Agrarian Crisis in India*, Oxford India.

RTFC, 2009, *Tool for Action*, New Delhi. Available at web:righttofoodindia.org.

Sen, Amartya, 2005, *The Argumentative Indian*, Allen Lane, New Delhi.

Shiva, Vandana, 1991, *Most Farmers in India are Women*, FAO, New Delhi.

Sujaya, C.P., 2006, *Climbing a Long Road: Women in Agriculture in India: Ten Years after Beijing*, M.S. Swaminathan Research Foundation, Chennai.

Swaminathan, M.S., 2005, *The Sons of the Soil*, in *The Hindu*, April 19.

Vepa, Swarna, 2004, Feminization of Agriculture and Marginalization of Their Economic Stake, *Economic and Political Weekly*, Vol. XL, No. 25 June 18–24.

World Bank, 2008, *World Development Report, The Agriculture for Development*, Washington, DC.

Annexure A

Key Terminology

Gender refers to socio-historic differences among men and women. Following Aggarwal (2003) we consider that 'gender ideologies and associated practices are culturally specific, historically variable and dialectically linked to property ownership and control.' Such differences are not biological but social in nature and therefore are not similar. There are discernible differences between men and women at the household, regional and national level.

Empowerment is understood as 'a process by which those who have been denied the ability to make strategic life choices acquire the ability to do so.' In relation to women in agriculture, empowerment is about changing *gender* relations in order to enhance *women's* ability to shape their lives. Thus, from an empowerment perspective, differences in how women and men are involved in decision-making, doing actual work and enjoying benefits are important dimensions. This study specifically covers aspects like awareness, beliefs and attitudes at different levels and their role in empowering women.

Contestation is an ongoing process that ultimately determines the gender relations at all levels: household, community, and national. In an overarching sense, women's needs, roles, and modes of behaviour are outcomes of day-to-day contestations. Contestation may take several forms, subtle and direct, like raising of voice, protests, arguments, boycott, not eating food, threats and physical assault.

In this report, the word ***State*** with capital S refers to all legal institutions that control social relations through means of rules, regulations, policies, programmes, schemes, et cetera. It thus includes all elected bodies, administrative units and their subsidiaries, enforcing authorities, and judicial bodies. The role of the state in defining, constructing and regulating social relations including gender relations is very important.

Agency is understood in the study as both the intention and the practice of taking action for one's own self-interest or the interests of others. This concept is important for understanding both contestation and empowerment.

Grass Ceiling is a term derived from more common 'glass ceiling' which is used to describe the 'unseen, yet unbreakable barriers that keep minorities and women from rising to the upper rungs of the corporate ladder.' Grass ceiling refers more precisely to a set of social, cultural and discriminatory barriers that prevent or discourage women farmers from deriving full benefit of their participation in agriculture.

Annexure B

Policy Directions by the National Commission for Women (NCW)

In 2006, the NCW was asked by the Swaminathan Commission, which was then preparing a Draft National Policy for Farmers, to provide certain inputs in the Draft Policy. NCW, with the help of a sub-committee of experts prepared an extensive note on the subject and sent it to the Swaminathan Commission.

However, after going through the finalised National Policy on Farmers 2007, NCW found that while some of the inputs provided by them had been accepted, the general nature of the policy document had marginalised many of their crucial concerns regarding women farmers and agricultural workers. So, NCW came out with a comprehensive document on the problems and needs of women in agriculture in the present time.

Given below are some of the most significant recommendations by NCW in Draft National Policy for Women in Agriculture which was submitted in April 2008.

1. In all legal measures on land rights, especially land reforms, there shall be special focus on the rights of women and single women-headed households including widows, abandoned and deserted women. All efforts shall be made to remove gender discriminatory provisions from all personal laws, both with regard to homestead as well as agricultural property.
2. Land titles will be held and recorded as joint pattas in the names of and with the signature and consent of both

the spouses. The Land Revenue Act shall be amended to include the provision of joint *pattas*. All land records shall be updated immediately after distribution of joint pattas and women shall be provided access to information about joint title to land and family property. Legal guidelines for independent access and control over joint pattas in case of dissolution of marriage shall be worked out. In case of dissolution of marriage, maintenance shall be worked out to include women's right to joint *patta*. The process of devolution of jointly held pattas shall be done in a manner which protects the right of daughters to parental property. Transfer and sale of any common agricultural or homestead land, whether owned privately or collectively, shall be done with the prior and explicit consent of both spouses.

3. All land acquisition for development and commercial activities shall be undertaken in accordance with land use plans prepared by state governments. Women shall be given adequate representation and hearing in the preparation of these plans and their needs and interests shall be taken into consideration.
4. In the context of the current food crisis primacy shall be given to the production of foodgrains by ensuring minimum support price, continuous and affordable supply of inputs, credit at minimum interests and the expansion of procurement, extension and other agricultural services.
5. Women's cooperatives shall be given priority in leasing or sale of uncultivated lands for agro-forestry or integrated and biological farming.
6. Technical and financial assistance shall be provided to adequate public investments in protective and micro-irrigation; land and soil conservation practices with a view to augment and increase the production of women farmers.
7. Family labour and the unpaid work of women in all farm and non-farm activities shall be recognized and accounted for in Gross Domestic Product. All policies,

research and evaluation activities of the state shall take note of such domestic and non-domestic activities supporting the agricultural sector.

8. Healthcare, childcare and old age pensions shall be provided to all women agricultural workers. All women agricultural workers shall be recognized and registered as workers for this purpose.
9. Seasonal and migrant women agricultural workers shall be accorded an appropriate status and given the same rights as other agricultural workers. Their rights shall be recognized in all policy statements, programmes and schemes.
10. Minimum and equal wages shall be enforced in all farm and non-farm activities in agriculture and allied activities. This shall be monitored by women representatives in panchayats.
11. Schemes shall be formed by state and central governments to subsidize and promote the formation of labour cooperatives and collective farming amongst women agricultural workers, especially the landless workers and marginal farmers.
12. The formation of cooperatives, group enterprises and SHG owned enterprises shall be promoted and subsidized in processing of agricultural produce.
13. Women agricultural workers shall be encouraged to undertake collective activities in non-farm sectors such as animal husbandry, forestry, and other activities through promotional schemes and subsidies.
14. Fertilizer and Manures: Public subsidies on chemical fertilizers and HYV seeds and pesticides shall be restored and additional support shall be given to women-headed households, especially in areas where farmer suicides have occurred. Production of vermi-compost and microbial fertilizers by women farmers and agricultural workers shall be promoted through SHG groups and SGSY schemes.
15. Seeds and Nurseries: Certified seeds shall be provided through the Krishi Vigyan Kendras. SHGs and SGSY

groups shall be used and supported for women's nurseries for preparation of plantation materials.

16. Bio Pesticides and Integrated Pest Management System: Local units owned and run by women's groups, particularly landless women, shall be set up for production of bio pesticides. Training, infrastructure and working capital for integrated pest management systems shall be provided by the state governments through different schemes and block development programmes.
17. Water and Electricity Supply for Agriculture and Allied Activities: Regulated and equitable supply of water and electricity shall be given to all women farmers at nominal rates. Single women-headed households, small and marginal farmers, and landless women workers from allied sectors shall be provided water and electricity free of cost.
18. Quantitative restrictions and import duties shall be reinstated to ensure that agricultural markets are protected for women in trade and retail of agriculture and allied products.
19. APMC Acts shall be strengthened to ensure that markets for small farmers and women agricultural workers are protected from unfair competition by monopolies and corporations in retail and procurement of produce.
20. Linkages of the Food Corporation of India (FCI) shall be made with women's SHGs for procuring agricultural produce from local mandis and areas where FCI does not have its own depots. Financial and infrastructural support shall be provided to these groups.
21. All-women mandis shall be set up locally so that women primary producers can directly market their produce in urban and rural areas.
22. Coarse grains, cereals, pulses, oilseeds and other essential produce necessary for the sustenance, health and nutrition of women and children shall be brought under the procurement system. A minimum support price shall be administered for them.
23. Policy and legislative support shall be provided to

protect women vegetable and food grain retailers from unfair competition by emerging monopolies.

24. A network of women-managed fair price shops shall be established to combat hunger and expand the scope and coverage of the public distribution system to all hamlets and villages.
25. Women kisan haats shall be set up for direct marketing and retail by women producers.
26. Financial and tax incentives shall be provided to women retailers so that they can compete better in the market.
27. The skills of women retailers shall be augmented through technical and credit support in all post harvest and processing operations. Women retailers shall be provided regular market information through field level schools and IT kiosks, and training in accounting, grading, packaging and other related activities. Technical assistance shall be given to upgrade the practices of women retailers so that they can provide value-added products at reasonable prices.
28. Debt Relief Commissions shall be formed at the state level in order to help indebted families facing agricultural distress, especially in areas where there are frequent farmer suicides.
29. Women-headed households, where women have been abandoned, deserted or rendered homeless because of farmers' suicides will be given special assistance to become debt free.
30. State governments shall take steps to regulate and give special subsidies to ease the debt of women farmers who have taken loans from moneylenders and micro finance institutions in the informal sector.
31. All institutions and individuals providing credit to rural households shall be registered at the block level. They shall have to provide credit at an interest rate that is comparable with and not higher than that of rural public sector banks.
32. Easy loans and subsidies shall be provided to aid the subsistence of women farmers and agricultural workers

in case of crop failure or natural disasters.

33. Access of women to rural credit shall be facilitated through simple documentation procedures where proof of residence should suffice to get a loan.
34. Diversified credit portfolios shall be developed to include consumption loans for education, health and other basic needs. This will be done on the basis of an integrated approach for overall credit requirements of the family.
35. SHGs who are willing to invest in agricultural marketing, post harvest operations and cooperative/group enterprises in allied sectors shall be given initial and working capital through soft loans.
36. A Gram Mahila Welfare Fund shall be formed in order to create common health, education and child care facilities at worker sites for women workers in agriculture and allied sectors.
37. Crop insurance schemes at nominal premium rates shall be universally implemented. Small and marginal farmers, and single women-headed households shall be provided insurance free of cost if they are unable.
38. Transparent monitoring systems shall be set up to periodically review the working and impact of the agricultural extension system and government schemes on women farmers and agricultural workers.
39. A cadre of women agricultural extension workers shall be created in order to ensure that women farmers have greater access to technology and knowledge that will reduce their labour time while increasing their productivity.
40. Women's knowledge of agriculture and allied sectors shall be recognized and integrated into the agricultural extension service.
41. Women SHGs shall be linked with the agricultural extension service in order to expand its scale and scope, particularly in areas of seed production, nurseries, application and production of bio fertilizers and pesticides, veterinary services, and post harvest operations.

42. Initiatives shall be taken to promote vocational education amongst rural women so that they can be better integrated into the agricultural extension system.
43. The linkages between agricultural universities and extension services shall be strengthened with particular reference to women's concerns.
44. A gender audit shall be done for all existing research and development programmes in agriculture and allied sectors. Evaluation of new experiments like biofarms, integrated and organic farming shall be done in order to gauge their impact on women's labour and work.
45. Science and technology organizations shall encourage and promote grassroots innovations and the development of need-based technologies which reduce the drudgery of women.
46. Women's knowledge of biodiversity in agriculture and allied sectors shall be recognized, integrated and upgraded in all research and development programmes. This will be done especially with respect to seed selection, storage, vegetable production, production of economic and medicinal plants, livestock rearing, food processing, nutrition, health, hygiene, sanitation and environmental protection.
47. The skills of women artisans shall be upgraded by undertaking programmes of creative grassroots innovations which blend modern day technologies with local knowledge and practices in production of seeds and agricultural inputs, renewable energy resources, and integrated nutrient and pest management.
48. The sustainable management and use of common property resources shall be upgraded through transfer and development of appropriate technologies. SHGs shall be linked to extension services in order to ensure appropriate technology transfer in areas of renewable energy, drinking water and the development of fuel and fodder.

Annexure C

Important Laws and Government Programmes/Schemes

There are several laws that are women-specific. Some of them are quite old and the latest one became operational in 2010. A select few that have bearing on the status of women are recounted here. These are not specific to our target group, women farmers, but are relevant for the status of women in general and are equally important for women in agriculture, if not more.

I: Some Select Laws

(a) The Protection of Women from Domestic Violence Act, 2005: The Act has been in effect since October 26, 2006. It is one of the most potent laws to prevent domestic violence as it includes severe penal provisions. It covers those women who are in relationship with the abuser and subjected to violence of physical, sexual, mental, verbal or emotional kind. In the face of widespread domestic violence prevalent in India, including in the study area as was noted in the previous chapter, its importance for women farmers is obvious.

(b) Hindu Succession Act, 1956: The original law provided equal share to daughters in the property of the parents but did not grant daughters share in the ancestral property. In 2005 this law was amended (The Hindu Succession (Amendment) Act, 2005 (39 of 2005) which came into effect from September 9, 2005). Gender discriminatory provisions in the Hindu Succession Act, 1956 have been changed. Now under Section 6 (i) the daughter of a coparcener cell by birth becomes a

coparcener in her own right in the same manner as the son; (ii) The daughter has the same rights in the coparcenary property as she would have had if she had been a son; (iii) The daughter is allotted the same share as is allotted to a son; (iv) The share of the pre-deceased son or a pre-deceased daughter shall be allotted to the surviving child of such a pre-deceased son or of such a pre-deceased daughter; (iv) The share of the pre-deceased child of a pre-deceased son or of a pre-deceased daughter shall be allotted to the child of such a pre-deceased child of the pre-deceased son or a pre-deceased daughter.

(c) The Prohibition of Child Marriage Act, 2006: prohibits child marriage. This act is extremely important for women as the child marriage affects girls/women adversely in several ways. Early marriage leading to early pregnancies is disastrous for women. It also takes a toll on them emotionally and psychologically.

(d) The Pre-natal Diagnostic Techniques (Regulation and Prevention of Misuse) Act, 1994: It was enacted and brought into operation from January 1, 1996, in order to check female foeticide. The Act prohibits determination and disclosure of the sex of the foetus. It also prohibits any advertisements relating to pre-natal determination of sex and prescribes punishment for its contravention. The person who contravenes the provisions of this Act is punishable with imprisonment and fines. The fact that the sex ratio in two of the three districts covered under the study has been precariously placed at around 850, the importance of the Act is beyond any debate.

(e) Mahatma Gandhi National Rural Employment Guarantee Act, 2005 (MNREGA): This Act guarantees employment within 15 days on demand to any household for 100 days at the rate of Rs 100/- per day within the village. More than one member can be enrolled for work. It applies universally to all those who desire. Says a group of men, *"NREGA is a good scheme as it provides work within the village; the rate is Rs 100 and it saves one from the humiliation of working for someone else."*

(f) The Right of Children to Free and Compulsory Education Act 2009 (RTE): it became operational in April 2010

and is very important as it ensures education to all the girls up to the age of 14 or middle class. Education as is well established is harbinger of change. In case of the current adult population, we find that the literacy rate among men is three times greater than women. Such discrimination would be tackled by this act.

It is true that legislation in itself does not mean anything. It is the social law that matters. But it is equally true that the legal right is vital and an effective tool for social actors. By using the tool a process of change can be initiated, furthered and consolidated.

(g) The Dowry Prohibition Act, 1961: The act is equally important given the problem of dowry and its adverse impact on the status of women. This act however has not been very effective on the ground. The NCW has recommended amendments in the Act which are pending with the Ministry of Law and Justice.

II: Select Important Programmes/Schemes

Like laws there are several schemes and programs that if implemented properly can have far-reaching impact on the status of women. Though there are innumerable programs/ schemes some of the important ones are:

(a) Public Distribution System (PDS): It has bearing on the women as it provides food security to poor farmer families. Our study reports that several women are suffering from food insecurity.

(b) Integrated Child Development Scheme (ICDS): It is a programme that provides nutritional support to pregnant and lactating women and adolescent girls. Two-thirds of Indian women suffer from anaemia. The ICDS provides supplementary nutrition to pregnant and lactating women and adolescent girls. It also provides nutrition and pre-school education to children in the age group six months to five years. The small and marginal women farmers need such a scheme for their well-being.

(c) Mid-Day Meal (MDM): This scheme ensures hot cooked meal to every child in school up to the class 8. It is also

beneficial as it helps retention in school of children from poor families including farmer families.

(d) Krishi Vigyan Kendra (KVK): These are the centres located at district level, one per district, to provide support exclusively to farmers. They play an important role in promoting modern scientific agricultural practices. They are responsible for extension services. However, their number is too small to cover all the farmers.

(e) National Rural Health Mission (NRHM): It is to ensure health including women's health in rural areas. For instance, to prevent maternal mortality and infant mortality, there is a special component of the scheme called *Janani Surakshya Yojana* to promote institutional delivery. This is a very useful scheme for women. Under this scheme a trained woman named ASHA is appointed in every village to promote health services.

(f) Minimum Support Price (MSP): There is a programme that ensures minimum prices for select food and non-food crops. This is especially to protect farmers from fluctuation of farm products and ensure minimum remuneration. However, several crops like vegetables and fruits are not covered under MSP. These are the perishable crops that are grown by small and marginal farmers.

(g) Kisan Card Yojana: In order to take care of the credit needs of the farmers this scheme has been initiated. Under this scheme, cards are given to farmers which they can use to access recurring credit.

(i) Crop Insurance: This is again a farm sector-specific scheme. It insulates farmers from natural and other unforeseen exigencies.

(j) Mahila Kisan Sashaktikaran Pariyojana (MKSP): In 2010-2011, the central government initiated MKSP for livelihood enhancement and vulnerability reduction of women as part of National Rural Livelihood Mission. It envisages empowering women in agriculture by making systematic investments to enhance their participation and productivity, as also create and sustain agriculture based livelihoods of rural women. The specific objectives include: (i) create sustainable

livelihood institutions around agriculture and allied activities (ii) create sector-specific geography-specific best package of practices and (iii) create a wide pool of community resource persons for scaling up livelihood interventions in the entire country. However, in its detailed roll out, the program doesn't lay any focus on defying the socio cultural and institutional challenges that overlook women's identity and presence as independent farmers. It doesn't address the structural barriers that have kept women marginalized for ages and are necessary to be addressed if gender equity is any goal.

All the above mentioned programmes are extremely important as they lead to betterment of women farmers directly or indirectly. We have mentioned these schemes only as examples, there are several more which can be beneficial for our target group.